PERSPECTIVES ON GIFTEDNESS
Sound Advice from Parents and Professionals

A Collection of Essays by GHF Writers

Edited by Ann Grahl

GHF Press

Perspectives on Giftedness
Sound Advice from Parents and Professionals
Managing author: Celi Trépanier
Interior design: Sztrecska Publishing
Cover art: Amanda Postma

Published by GHF Press, an imprint of GHF Learners
ghflearners.org

ISBN: 978-1-7375161-0-1

This collection is for all of the gifted individuals we are honored to support and who, in return, enrich our lives and show us the full meaning of the gifted experience. To you, we extend our appreciation and dedication.

CONTENTS

ACKNOWLEDGMENTS

GHF Press is the publishing imprint of GHF Learners, which is dedicated to providing learning opportunities and resources to all members of the gifted population as well as to the families, educators, and professionals who support those individuals. To take advantage of all GHF has to offer, visit ghflearners.org. We thank GHF Learners for supporting publication of this compilation and all of the many volunteers who work tirelessly to make GHF a go-to resource for the gifted community.

We also extend our appreciation to the authors, who generously donated essays for inclusion within. The work of these writers is worth further exploration, and we encourage you to read the "About the Authors" section and to follow them online at their respective websites, blogs, and social media pages. We are especially grateful to Celi Trépanier, managing author of *Perspectives*, for her vision and her valuable contributions to this project.

You likely noticed the unique cover art—particularly if you are holding a print version of the book. We appreciate Amanda Postma's creativity and perspective in providing that original artwork.

We further express our heartfelt thanks to you, our readers, for allowing us to share a bit of your journey.

Finally, to the gifted and those supporting them: We see you. We feel you. We applaud you. And we thank you.

INTRODUCTION

The world of gifted advocacy is a welcoming place encompassing a variety of individuals with unique voices—parents who have been there, educators who are working to get it right, and psychologists and other professionals who understand the rich complexity that is so often part and parcel of giftedness. The more you read of their personal stories and take in their shared wisdom, the more you feel as if you've been invited into a gathering of friends.

This collection of essays from some of the most highly sought after and widely recognized writers in the gifted community offers perspective and guidance on an array of topics. Each of these authors brings a distinctive viewpoint, and you're certain to discover among their contributions an experience to which you can relate, a new way of looking at something, or a bit of advice that makes you respond, "Hey, I never thought of that."

As each part of the book unfolds, you'll find yourself comfortably situated among confidants freely discussing all aspects of giftedness—from its characteristics, to its impact in childhood and education, to the twice-exceptional experience, to adulthood. So, grab your favorite beverage, take a nice cushy seat, and join us as we explore the many facets of being gifted.

Part One: Giftedness Is

There's no denying it: "Gifted" is a loaded term, with multiple definitions causing ample confusion. It can be a contradictory label. On the one hand, do we see giftedness as a blessing—a present wrapped in privilege tied with a bow of bliss? Or do we, on the other hand, more accurately view it as one's humanly imperfect essence based on the wiring with which they're born.

In our eagerness to precisely discern *what* it is, we often overlook *who* it is. And all of our defining or, worse yet, judging doesn't begin to paint the picture nearly as completely as the gifted individuals themselves. As we've muddled through finding a concrete, be-all and end-all definition, there is one that continues to stand out as coming close to illuminating the gifted experience—that of the Columbus Group:

> Giftedness is asynchronous development in which advanced cognitive abilities and heightened intensity combine to create inner experiences and awareness that are qualitatively different from the norm. This asynchrony increases with higher intellectual capacity. The uniqueness of the gifted renders them particularly vulnerable and requires modifications in parenting, teaching, and counseling in order for them to develop optimally.[1]

In "Giftedness Is," we peel back the labels and take a look at the stickiness of what giftedness means and how we talk about it—the details and the big picture. And, here and in the remainder of the book, we'll always adhere to one truth: Giftedness starts and ends with an individual—a child who grows into an adult but never outgrows being gifted.

Part Two: Gifted Beginnings

And so this is where it begins. It meaning the struggles, the amazement, the revelations, the fears, the advocacy, and the realization that raising a gifted child is a different sort of parenting—nothing at all like what you were expecting and definitely not the sort of child-rearing found in any parenting book.

As the parent of a gifted child, you recognize within the first years of your child's life that most other parents just aren't in the same boat as you. In fact, it can feel like you're in a boat in the middle of the ocean without a life preserver or a paddle. Mayday, mayday, mayday!

This is where the contributions in "Gifted Beginnings" come to the rescue—the authors throw a life preserver and a couple of paddles and invite you aboard their ship of gifted families who are a lot like yours. They offer support, validation, and just enough navigation to empower you to chart your own course for raising your unique gifted child.

And the first port of call—education.

Part Three: Gifted Gets Schooled

Education seems the prime focus of many parents during the first 18 years of their child's life. For the parents of gifted children, education can prove to be a contentious issue, often becoming the proverbial thorn in their side. Traditional schooling, whose fundamental structure is teaching a classroom of students effectively and efficiently, can fail to provide the learning environment gifted children need.

These youngsters have unique learning needs that can confound both parents and teachers. Unlike the gifted student stereotype of a pupil who excels across the board, these children, in reality, can be a few grade levels ahead in some subjects and average or below average in others. Gifted kids may not excel in all areas; but, in the areas in which they do excel, their education needs to meet them where they are and match their pace of learning.

Information is vital for parents during their child's elementary and middle school years. And support from parents who have traveled this path before serves to bolster the confidence of bewildered parents of gifted children who face an educational system that often neglects their child's learning needs. In "Gifted Gets Schooled," you'll obtain some much-needed support as you seek to secure the best education possible for your gifted child.

Feeling supported is even more crucial if you happen to have a twice-exceptional child.

Part Four: 2eeek!

What is twice exceptional, you may ask? Well, one of our favorite definitions is "exceptionally gifted and an exceptional pain in the ... uh ... backside." Wait, we can't say that? Okay then.

"Gifted plus something that interferes with the giftedness" tends to be the most recognized definition. That *something* can be a learning or physical disability, slow processing speed, ADHD, autism spectrum disorder, anxiety, depression, mental illness, sensory processing disorder, central auditory processing disorder, dyslexia, dysgraphia, dyscalculia—the list goes on. Oftentimes, it's not just one "e" in play but several plus the interactions between those.

Twice exceptionality is hard to determine and hasn't been recognized or accepted for very long, because it is hiding in plain sight. The giftedness compensates for the challenges and the challenges mask the giftedness. It's overwhelming.

The authors in "2eeek!" generously share their expertise on twice exceptionality, including the *joys* (no, not really) of asynchronous development. It's our hope that in the near future, 2e will be more widely recognized and supported, with much less exhaustion all around.

Whew, there's a lot to know about giftedness and gifted kids. But, surely by the time gifted children grow up, they have things figured out, right? Ah, if only.

Part Five: Gifted Grows Up

In actuality, adult giftedness is tricky. As we age, it can become harder to define and explore what it means to live as a gifted soul. And having any labels attached to us at this late date can be a sticking point. But thinking in terms of Paula Prober's rainforest mind metaphor can help.[2]

We can think of people as ecosystems—some are meadows, some deserts, some volcanoes, and some rainforests. All are valuable and necessary. The rainforest is just the most complex: intense, intelligent, colorful, multilayered, full of life, curious, and misunderstood. Viewing giftedness in this way may make it easier to see it in ourselves. So, while we may be uncomfortable having the gifted label applied to us, we may be open to accepting our lush rainforest minds.

And this self-acceptance is important. The gifted traits that we embodied as children follow us into adulthood. We may be highly sensitive, extremely lonely, frustrated in the workplace, or driven to create a better world. We may feel pressure to meet our highest expectations or feel like failures if we make even the smallest mistake. As parents of gifted children, we may be overcome with intense love for these young ones and yet we may be frightened by the ways in which we see ourselves in them.

Addressing our own needs, desires, unhealthy patterns, and unresolved issues from our early years can make all the difference for our children. Understanding what it means to be a gifted adult benefits everyone. Making the time for self-examination, self-awareness, and self-love is not selfish. Quite the opposite. It allows us to flourish and then nourish those around us. It is what our children, our families, our communities, and our planet so desperately need.

In "Gifted Grows Up," we'll unravel more of the complexity of the adult gifted mind and share some, perhaps relatable, life experiences of those making the journey through adulthood while simultaneously coming to terms with the lingering impacts of growing up gifted.

In the end, each of us has our own perspective. Though we may share common characteristics, we are all our own characters. Our hope is that the essays in this compilation help you to write your own story and guide you and your children as you pursue your lifelong treks as gifted individuals. We wish you safe and enlightening travels.

PART ONE
Giftedness Is

I demand more. I demand more for my son, for your child, for all of our gifted children struggling in this world—against poor educational fit, against bullying, against a society that thinks these children are not gifted unless they produce and produce in volume. Gifted is. Period. No ifs, ands, or buts about it.

—Jen Merrill

Gifted *vs* Gifted

KATHLEEN HUMBLE

What do we mean when we say gifted? It seems like a
simple question. It's not.

See, the first thing anyone notices about giftedness is the wildly different
definitions. Is it medical? Psychological? Educational? Gifted changes from
country to country, district to district, and even school to school. It's head-
scratchingly confusing. It doesn't make sense ... and it's easy to ask, "Is gifted
even real? Is it all made up?"

Why Is It So Difficult to Define?

A few weeks back, I had a conversation with a highly qualified educational
expert that really clarified the issue. We disagreed. She showed me her journal
references. I showed her mine. And I discovered something. Something that
should have been blindingly obvious. Something that had nagged me for a
really long time, particularly when I read a journal paper that felt "fuzzy" on
definitions. Some articles even seemed to lack basic reproducibility (not having
enough information for another group to repeat the same experiment/study).

Eventually, she said, "Well, these things (I was talking about) might apply to
a small subgroup of children..." (or words to that effect).

That's when the lightning bolt hit: *Her definition of gifted was not just different
from mine; we weren't talking about the same group of kids.*

When we talk gifted, what are we talking about? High IQ? High achieving?
Behavioral differences? Neurological wiring?

We *have* to start here: What do we mean when we say gifted?

Educationally Gifted (E-Gifted)

When educators talk about giftedness, particularly in journals, they generally
consider children who achieve in the top 10% in classroom assignments

or school assessments.[1] There is no IQ test or consideration of behavioral characteristics. There is only one criterion—high achievement.

The kids who fall into the E-gifted category are generally well behaved. They like learning at school, are socially well adjusted, and are usually reasonably well liked. They have fewer mental health problems. Dedicated and hardworking, they go on to pursue high-achieving careers, acquire greater-than-average numbers of degrees, and write more journal articles. They are also more likely to climb to the top rungs of whatever professional ladder they choose. These individuals are relatively easy for teachers to spot in a class.

Psychologically Gifted (P-Gifted)

P-gifted children are primarily defined by IQ tests. They will have an IQ score in the top 2.1% of the population, or two standard deviations above the norm or average score. (For the Wechsler Intelligence Scale for Children [WISC], this would be a score of 130+.) Children with a diagnosed disability affecting their communication or motor skills may, instead, have some subscores in the top ~2% and an average score (if it can be calculated) at least one standard deviation above average (for the WISC, this would be 115+).[2]

These children have a higher likelihood of problems in school due to a poor educational fit. They are more likely to be referred for testing for disabilities (even if none are present). Most will have behavioral characteristics that are often described as overexcitabilities, which can also be explained using the Five Factor Model of Personality as an overabundance of Openness.[3,4] There is also a much higher chance that they will have sensory processing issues significant enough for them to be classified as having a sensory processing disorder.[5]

They are not all high achieving. They are present in all populations and at all socioeconomic levels; however, if they are from a minority group or a poor background, they are unlikely to be identified.[6]

This group includes those who are more likely to show up at testing centers or in the offices of psychologists and counselors. From the small amount of data collected, they are much more likely to be homeschooled.[7]

Combination E-Gifted and P-Gifted

The third group comprises both E-gifted and P-gifted individuals. These children have a high IQ score and are also high achieving. This is the group every longitudinal study of giftedness I have seen has focused on. (I have read through five of the most comprehensive.) This is also the group that neurologists like to study when they do brain scans of how gifted brains work or genetic studies on inheritance. This group fits nicely into all the definitions of giftedness, members are easy to find, *and* it provides a repeatable, reproducible study group. You might say that these individuals represent the medical model of giftedness.

Twice Exceptional (2e)

The 2e group is a subset of the P-gifted group. (If they are high achieving but not P-gifted, then they are high-achieving special needs or disabled children, *not* 2e.) A small number of these children may end up being labeled as both E-gifted and P-gifted, but most of them will be missed and not even identified as P-gifted. They will almost certainly *not* receive the accommodations they need in school and are drastically more likely to drop out or be homeschooled. (According to the minimal amount of data we have, in my state of Victoria, Australia, while only 1 in 200 children is homeschooled, 1 in 7 2e children is homeschooled.[8])

Why Does This Matter?

But why does all this matter? Why is it important to know which group we are talking about? *It's important because the educational, social, emotional, and medical needs of these groups vary greatly.*

E-Gifted Children

E-gifted children (except those who are also P-gifted) thrive on the challenges they get in classrooms. Teachers are usually able to successfully differentiate for these students' needs if the latter require extension. These students very rarely need acceleration and almost never need radical acceleration—indeed, it can occasionally be harmful, as it increases their stress levels as they try to keep up. Radical acceleration can also cause behavioral problems, as these children may not be emotionally or socially able to blend in with the older children.

P-Gifted Children

There is very little, if any, large-scale longitudinal data regarding P-gifted children. We have no idea how they turn out. We have no idea about their mental health or achievement profiles on a large scale. But there are many case studies and individual profiles, which indicate the following:

◇ higher-than-average risk of dropping out of school
◇ higher-than-average risk of mental health problems

✧ risk of both misdiagnosis and missed diagnosis with possible co-occurring disabilities

✧ potentially higher-than-average risk of going to prison

These children need acceleration. And highly to profoundly gifted children need radical acceleration—not because they could achieve at a higher rate if accelerated, but because, without it, they are more likely to develop mental health problems, particularly unhealthy, clinically significant levels of crippling perfectionism.[9] Differentiation within a classroom seldom works, as it is rarely done the way they need to learn. This is because it's designed for E-gifted children.

If they don't end up in an educational environment that meets their needs, there are documented lifelong problems.[10] If they also feel unsafe and unwelcome, it's even worse. Most P-gifted kids don't understand how differently from average they think, which causes social problems. They have an intense focus on justice and fair play and a desire for exactness and accuracy that can be mistaken for autism (though there is a growing body of scientific data to say that there is some link—possibly genetic—between some P-gifted children and autism).[11]

Combination E-Gifted and P-Gifted Children

Children who are both E-gifted and P-gifted will do fine in a regular classroom with differentiation but, if not accelerated, will be less well adapted over their lifetime. If they are accelerated, they will have an even higher-achieving profile and will gain more degrees on average, publish more papers, and climb higher within their chosen profession.[12] There may be some mental health issues if they are not accelerated to a level equal to their ability. This is particularly true for highly to profoundly gifted children within the high-achieving group. (I define highly to profoundly gifted as three standard deviations above average on an IQ test.[13])

2e Children

For 2e children, the previously discussed challenges can be made worse by the way special needs children are treated within the educational system. It's an unhealthy clash between ableism and tall poppy syndrome; that is, if they are even identified (which they probably won't be). Schools invariably favor working only on deficits, even if acceleration removes most of the problems seen in the classroom. These children can also have accommodations for disabilities removed if they jump from the P-gifted to the Combination group (that is, start becoming high achieving).[14]

Conclusion

I think it is vitally important to understand exactly what we are talking about when we talk about gifted kids. Before we can make decisions on how to help them, we need to understand exactly which group of kids we're talking about. If we don't, we'll have the same circular arguments again and again. We'll fling facts, not listen, and get nowhere. I know what that's like. I've done it—a lot.

No one is arguing some children must suffer and be squashed. Or that failing and traumatizing some children is the price we must pay for other children to do well. But that, too often, is where the conversation ends up—no matter which side we're on in the giftedness definition debate. Instead, I think we should pause. Revisit the assumptions. Reassess whether we're even discussing the same thing. And realize that we're actually looking for the same outcome but for very different groups of children.

Those Gifted Code Words

JEN MERRILL

So, how do you say gifted?

Once I know a person, or a situation, I say it with my talk hole. The one under my nose. The one I also eat with, play flute with, let loose the occasional whistle from, and on whose lips I test drive a new ChapStick. I say gifted. I say twice exceptional. I say it's not achievement but wiring. I say it's who a person is and not what they accomplish. I don't stutter. I don't use air quotes (my god I hate seeing "gifted"). I say gifted without shame or embarrassment because I know it's not anything resembling a gift most of the time. Or, rather, if someone bought me a gift like gifted, I'd have a hard time deciding if I should return it or kindly suggest the giver shove it where the sun don't shine.

But before I know a person or if I'm new to a situation? Code words. Lots and lots of code words:

♦ challenging—needed an educational situation other than what the school could provide

♦ very bright

♦ deep thinker but doesn't test well

♦ easily overwhelmed by sensory input

♦ makes unusual and profound connections

♦ not like other kids

If I'm talking to a parent, by then, they've also used various code words, we both realize we're talking to a kindred spirit, and we can drop the facade and go for wine. If I'm talking to a professional who is involved with my kid … well … that really depends on the professional. Some give off the "don't talk to me about gifted" vibe; others are more open to the wide neuropsychological

12

variety that is the human race. I read the other person as we talk and I choose my words based on the tone of the conversation. And sometimes I just don't give a damn and say whatever I like.

Gifted is a terrible word for these outlier kids and their outlier parents—giftedness is not a gift from the universe and there are days when I would send it back if I could. But it's the only word we have; it's the only word that's recognized (however poorly) for this right-hand-side-of-the-bell-curve life. And it's an unfortunate word for what it describes. I think if more parents of gifted kids (not necessarily high-achieving kids) were open and honest about the struggles and complexities of raising gifted kids and flat out owned that word … well then, maybe, there would be less stigma attached to it.

Probably not. So, my talk hole will keep speaking the words "gifted" and "twice exceptional," loudly and proudly. They're all we have and I refuse to be shamed out of using them. I'll just keep my code words handy, you know, just in case.

I'm Not a (Fill-in-the-Blank); I'm Gifted

STACIE BROWN McCULLOUGH

Real Life

The dentist asks my seven-year-old son what grade he's in. He stares at the wall behind her and lets out a deep sigh.

Does she mean what grade level am I on and, if so, which subject? Should I say I'm homeschooled? Why does she want to know? Does she even know what homeschooling is about? Am I gonna have to explain that to her?

The swim coach heard he's smart and holds his fingers up. "How many is this?" He gives another blank stare.

Does he need help figuring it out? Is he playing a joke on me? What does this have to do with swimming? Doesn't he know I know fractions and chemistry already? Should I tell him everything I know so he doesn't ask me these types of questions again?

Those poor unsuspecting adults. They didn't just walk right into it, they ran up cheering, hit their heads, and fell smack on their faces into it.

My son couldn't turn off the questions. He couldn't stop thinking and analyzing to "just answer a simple question," because, to him, it wasn't a simple question. Nothing is simple when you can't stop thinking, when there are so many variables to consider.

And that's why the outpouring of words that followed flabbergasted each inquisitor. Of course, he answered all the questions, even the ones they didn't ask. My son is not an extrovert, not an overachiever, not a know-it-all, not a (fill-in-the-blank). He's gifted.

More Something

Because my son and I constantly process information, we can't Just. Stop. Nor do we want to even if we could.

14

Gifted is a different way of thinking, a different way of behaving, a different way of learning. We're not all "Sheldons," but we are all a little more. We seem to be alike only in the ways we are different from others. That's why it's so difficult to determine giftedness without testing, especially in those of us who are twice exceptional, or 2e (gifted with a learning disability). But you know. As a parent, *you just know.*

Because we're gifted, we can appear insensitive, aloof, like know-it-alls or show-offs. Paradoxically, it can make us appear hypersensitive, needy, or slow. We can be complete opposites, sometimes at the same time. We don't all look alike. We don't all think alike. We don't all have the same quirks (or overexcitabilities).[15]

Giftedness doesn't make us more special, or more important, or higher achieving, necessarily. It doesn't make us more of anything. It just makes us *more*—intense, sensitive, pensive, energetic, spirited, creative, argumentative, impulsive (to name a few possibilities)—just *more*.

Homeschool Struggles

I struggled for the last couple years homeschooling my son because I didn't know our giftedness could be so similar yet so different. I questioned everything—from his giftedness to his behavior to my parenting to my own giftedness, and everything in between. In my tiny rural community, it seemed no one else was in a similar position or had similar circumstances. We "just don't talk about those things."

To top it off, at the beginning, I barely knew anyone who homeschooled. If I had known someone else with experience homeschooling, or I had been part of a supportive community of homeschoolers with gifted kids, such as that found with GHF Learners, I might not have struggled so long with coming to grips with my son's giftedness. I might have had a better handle on what it means to be 2e. I might have spent more time celebrating strengths and relishing joys instead of anxiously agonizing over every aspect of our gifted/2e life.

Real life can be a real struggle for parents raising gifted/2e children and confronting the vast unknown variables of alternative education. Choosing an atypical method of educating an atypical child means really real life rushes head-on into the intensity, the sensitivity, and the moreness of giftedness. The struggle of and with mores is real, and you are not … fill-in-the-blank. You're likely gifted too.

Dealing with the Difficulties of Giftedness—One Day at a Time

BETSY SPROGER

My husband and I learned our daughter is twice exceptional (2e, gifted with a learning challenge) when she was very young. As she grew, we found ways to deal with some of the typical issues associated with her giftedness, along with the sensory processing disorder, attentional issues, and anxiety with which she struggled. My daughter is now a successful college graduate. In this essay, I am looking back to when the difficulties of her giftedness first arose and the steps her father and I took to help her—and us— work through them.

The Challenge: Sleep

As a little one, our daughter took hours to get to sleep. Learning to settle her excited intense mind was a challenge for sure. A consistent bedtime routine, with bath and story time, helped some, but still seemingly each night she would take more than two hours to settle down and go to sleep. Things gradually got better as we tried a number of approaches to help. And, by the time she was in sixth grade, her inability to fall asleep was much less of an issue.

What Helped

Bedtime Routine

Following a similar bedtime routine each night helped. We provided lots of books and favorite quiet activities so that she could play on her own in her room. As a preschooler, she learned to stay in her room after story time and usually played herself to sleep. This gave her father and I some time to relax in the next room after our own hectic days while remaining available to her if needed. Gradually things improved.

16

Breathing Exercises and Relaxation Techniques

Breathing exercises, child-oriented relaxation recordings, and favorite music also proved useful. We taught our young one how to breath from the diaphragm, making it a game and doing it together while lying on the floor. We each put a toy on our stomach and practiced making the toy go up and down using our diaphragm.

Her father and I gradually learned to accept that this was our new normal: For many years, it just took our daughter more time to drift off.

The Challenge: Intensities and Anxiety

Our daughter had many intense feelings, along with a multitude of questions, and she required a lot of attention. This made me one exhausted mama—to the point where both she and I needed naps!

What Helped

Homeschooling

Learning at home proved beneficial, as our daughter could delve deeply into subjects or be quite active, neither of which she could do in a classroom setting. We always kept books and craft supplies around, available for her use anytime. When she was a preschooler, we went through tons of cardboard and tape. It was such a joy to see her creations!

Maintaining Routine

Structuring our daughter's time helped her to learn to manage her intensities. We developed a predictable schedule. She could anticipate what was going to happen next, and that knowledge eased her anxiety. We also used breaks, reading quietly or viewing a favorite movie from the library, to help settle her down when necessary.

Afternoon Naps or Solitary Play

Napping in the afternoon was essential, as both my daughter and I required the rest. When she no longer needed a nap, we switched to her engaging in quiet playtime in her bedroom. This solitary play provided comfort for her and allowed me to practice self-care so that I could function better and help her to as well.

Using Blankets

Blankets are great for deep pressure, to help calm the nerves. Have you ever heard of "making a burrito" with a blanket? This can really help a child who is overloaded, overstimulated, or very anxious. To do so, spread out a blanket on the couch. Then ask your child to sit on it and help them wrap each side of the blanket across their lap, in effect making a burrito with them snuggled into it. This was my preschooler's favorite calming mechanism. We used a regular blanket, not a weighted one, and did not wrap it tightly. This was done for short periods (a few minutes) whenever our daughter desired it. Sometimes, she preferred simply being rolled up gently in a blanket. Ah, the comfort of that softness and warmth.

Baths

When our daughter was young, we had lots of toys available for play in the tub along with items that she could stick on the wall. This kept her interested in bathing longer, and the warm water provided a calming effect. Baths were not just for her, though, and I often tried to find time at night for a long, soothing bath myself, as my husband took over the bedtime routine most evenings.

Though our daughter's intensities could be challenging, they also invited us to share in her intense joy and passions along the way.

The Challenge: Sensory Issues

Sensory issues are quite common among gifted kids. My daughter was a sensory seeker, always wanting vestibular input—spinning, running, twirling, jumping, doing headstands off the couch, etc. I have a background in occupational therapy so I was comfortable finding the sensory activities that she required. And our couches outlasted all of the handsprings and tumbling!

She also needed lots of deep pressure input. In addition, she reacted to tags on clothing and to those wardrobe articles that were restrictive. She was tactile defensive and loud noises bothered her as well—though simply acknowledging the latter was often comfort enough: "Oh, that was a siren. I know you don't like noises like that."

What Helped

Gymnastics

Our daughter was a natural gymnast!

So, she took part in the parks department toddler play and tumbling classes, which were very helpful. Preschool gymnastics led to more through the years. Having gymnastics skills meant that she could use them to take active breaks whenever she needed to, to calm herself or to exert energy.

Whether it was tumbling, cartwheels, or headstands, I encouraged it. We even made a simple gymnastics floor in her bedroom. Gymnastics became a favorite activity all the way through high school and that led to a welcome side effect—increased self-esteem.

I loved watching her gymnastics meets and seeing her on the balance beam performing her routines. But paid classes are not mandatory; that is just what we chose to do. Any traditional playground with swings and a merry-go-round can work well too.

We also invested in a simple plastic spinner, on which our daughter could sit and spin. As she grew older, we acquired a desk chair to spin on, a small inside trampoline for use during winter, a large exercise ball to bounce, and a swing and large trampoline for outside use in warmer weather. And, of course, we made many trips to the local park.

Some families look for a pediatric occupational therapist and work with that professional on sensory integration therapy.

Clothing Adjustments

We made an effort to adjust our daughter's wardrobe, avoiding jeans and tight clothing and instead opting for sweatpants, sweatshirts, and t-shirts—and removing tags. Note that by the time middle school rolled around, jeans had gained popularity in our house and the desire for sweatpants began to wane. Oh, the fun of shopping with my daughter for jeans for the first time!

The Challenge: Anxiety

Our daughter struggled with anxiety, desiring predictability and needing to know what was going to happen next—where we were going, who we would see, etc.

What Helped

Predictable Routine

We gave our daughter as much control as possible, offering two or three options. We engaged in lots of play—at home and at the park; taught her self-calming exercises, including deep breathing; encouraged goofing off and being silly; allowed for downtime, which included quiet reading or listening to audio books; and offered soothing baths. Our focus was on reinforcing independent development while being there for her.

Using fidgets, small items to play with, was a great help when homeschooling, especially when verbal directions or explanations were given. As our daughter became more confident, her anxieties lessened.

The Challenge: Competitive Tendencies and Perfectionism

Our daughter exhibited competitive tendencies and perfectionism, the latter to which I was also prone. Together, we developed strategies that alleviated these issues.

As our daughter has grown, competitiveness has become a positive force. She has learned to balance her competitive spirit with other facets of her life, such as self-care, all while pushing herself toward achievement of her dreams.

What Helped

Thinking Games

When our daughter was young, we often let her win board games. Then we began obtaining games that required a lot of thinking—cognitive games such as chess. She was often so distracted by the thinking process that she forgot to focus on winning. And I have many fond memories of my daughter and husband playing all sorts of games together.

Humor

A sense of humor was another weapon in our arsenal. We didn't put pressure on victory and made light of losing. When my daughter was young, we had fun practicing making mistakes so that it became like a game. Making mistakes on purpose decreased the negative feelings around slipping up.

Summary

Many of the issues discussed in the previous sections were remedied by the time our daughter entered high school. Throughout the process of working through these challenges, we honored our daughter's achievements and, at the same time, tried to help her find and maintain balance by teaching her to follow her heart, build in self-care, and give herself permission to make lots of mistakes. And us too!

Gifted Is

JEN MERRILL

It's more than likely you don't know the name Aaron Swartz; before his life was prematurely halted, I didn't either. But, if you've ever read anything on a feed reader, he's why. Among many other things, he helped create the RSS feed. When he was 14.

In 2013, at the age of 26, he hanged himself.

He suffered from depression and was being prosecuted by the U.S. Attorney for illegally downloading five million academic articles from a subscription service. He believed deeply that all information should be available for free. With a little googling, you can learn all the details. But that's not what impacted me at the time or why, to this day, when I think about Swartz, I find myself shaken and red eyed. Rick Perlstein of *The Nation* wrote of his friend:

> I remember always thinking that he always seemed too sensitive for this world we happen to live in, and I remember him working so mightily, so heroically, to try to bend the world into a place more hospitable to people like him, which also means hospitable to people like us.[16]

And I sob. I sob for my son, my incredibly sensitive twice-exceptional son, who can become distraught beyond words at the news of loss (such as when he heard that our beloved pediatrician in Colorado had died shortly before the day Aaron Swartz took his own life). I sob for all of our gifted and twice-exceptional children, fighting their way through their demons as the world around them actively strives to strike them down. I sob for us parents, struggling day after day to help our complex children navigate this world, even as we rail against the weight and unfairness of the burden. I sob for Aaron Swartz and for the pain his parents likely still feel.

This young man, whom I never met and had not heard of before his death, was obviously gifted—perhaps profoundly. Based on what I've read, he loved life and learning and creating solutions to problems no one yet knew they had. I didn't know I needed an RSS feed reader until I used one; now I can't imagine not using one daily. I think I would have liked Aaron Swartz; he reminds me of my own son.

People, what are we doing to our best and brightest? I still mourn this young man because he is … he is the child we're raising now. Every time I read Perlstein's observation of his friend, "he always seemed too sensitive for this world we happen to live in," my heart breaks anew for our gifted sons and daughters. They are not gifted because they can do higher level math, or write complex computer code, or read and understand and discuss Chaucer. They are gifted because that is who they are. They are not, I repeat *not*, the product of their talents. Giftedness is not always a gift; too often, it's a burden. To carry that burden alone, seeing and tasting and feeling the world differently while being lauded only for what you produce, for what you give to the world…

Gifted children and adults are not gifted for what they do; they just are. And it is dangerous and negligent to forget that. To focus solely on talents and eminence reduces a person's very being down to "what have you done for me (society) lately" and "you're only gifted if what you produce is worthwhile (to society)." And that's not good enough. I demand more. I demand more for my son, for your child, for all of our gifted children struggling in this world— against poor educational fit, against bullying, against a society that thinks these children are not gifted unless they produce and produce in volume. Gifted is. Period. No ifs, ands, or buts about it.

I mourn Aaron Swartz, a young man I didn't know. But I know a lot of young gifted kids, and I pray that I never have to mourn them. We can do better for our children, and we must.

Ode to the Suckiness
of Being Gifted

HEATHER BOORMAN

Writing this essay was a bit of a struggle. I started and restarted, deleted and backspaced more times than I care to count. Maybe it's because I've procrastinated (as usual) and am writing this after a long day, at a time when I'd rather be asleep in my bed. Maybe it's because my brain has felt out of words for the past two hours. But, more likely, it's because I have too many ideas. I haven't been able to choose just one difficulty about being gifted. I really don't think I'm that pessimistic or cynical, but there often seem to be far more challenges around being gifted than not. I remember being a young child and wishing I could just shut my brain off. I remember being a young woman and wishing I didn't have so many options in front of me. I've been an adult and wished to be ignorant. Being gifted is complicated and those complications come with difficulty. I long for simple. Except when I don't. So, in lieu of being able to pick just one struggle of being gifted, I've opted to create a list. And, because my brain simultaneously wants simplicity and challenge, I'm creating my list as an acrostic poem:

> **T**urning off your mind is impossible
> **H**aving multiple interests and goals to pursue can be daunting
> **E**xpectations set by others can be maddening
>
> **S**o few people understand what giftedness entails
> **U**nderstanding the first time but having to hear it explained seven
>   more times is torture
> **C**hewing sounds are magnified and disgusting
> **K**ids don't like the smartest kid in class
> **I**ntense living is *intense*
> **N**oticing *everything* is exhausting

Explaining how you got your answer when you can't explain it to
   yourself is exasperating
Sitting through meetings is unbearable
Stumbling upon like-minded, similarly wired individuals is rare

Overthinking, overanalyzing, and overplanning is *overwhelming*
Finding creative, intellectual outlets is vital but not always a priority

Bullies like to pick on the smart kid
Emotions are HUGE
Inefficiency can be infuriating
Never meeting one's own desire for perfection is frustrating
Giftedness does *not* equal high achieving, but everyone thinks it does

Growing up is wildly asynchronous
Idealism causes unrealistic expectations
Finding the balance between being challenged and not overwhelmed
   is a struggle
Thinking big thoughts and asking big questions isn't always
   welcomed
Empathy can be awesome but totally draining
Daughters and sons tend to be gifted too.

I'm Not Gifted. I'm Just Weird.

PAULA PROBER

You'd think that gifted people would know how smart they are. You'd think that gifted individuals would find life to be smooth and easy. You'd think that gifted folks would feel superior and judgmental of all nongifted humans everywhere.

Nope. No way. Not the ones I know. And I've known a lot of them. I'm *that* old. (My former middle school students are turning 50. Yeah. Old. OK. Old-ish.)

Granted, I work with a particular variety of gifted souls: the rainforest-minded (RFM). Not all gifted folks are the RFM type. Some can be cognitively advanced but not highly sensitive or empathetic. Some can be very academic and scholarly but not have multipotentiality. So yes. Maybe some of the non-RFM gifted know how smart they are, find life to be easy, and are judgmental. Maybe.

But they weren't in my classroom when I was a teacher in the mid-1970s and 1980s. They haven't been in my counseling office for the past 25+ years. The RFM folks I've known will tell you: *I'm not gifted. I'm just weird.* And they will struggle—with sensitivities, injustice, decisions, choices, achievement, school, relationships, communication, emotions, careers, belonging, parenting, anxiety, depression, perfectionism, guilt, politics, climate change deniers, conspicuous consumption, not enough time to read all of the books ever written, and so much else.

And that's if they grew up in a healthy family.

If you throw dysfunctional family into the mix, it gets even more complicated.

So, if you have a rainforest mind, or if you love someone who does or work with someone who does or teach those who do, it's time to get out of denial.

It matters. Why?

It matters because everyone will benefit if RFM humans understand why they struggle and what to do about it. It matters because RFM parents are raising RFM kids. If the parents know who they are, they'll be better able to support their children. It matters because educators, psychotherapists, doctors, and other professionals will stop misdiagnosing their clients and will become more effective practitioners.

It matters because we all need the intelligence, compassion, creativity, and sensitivity that RFM beings share with us—just like we all need our tropical rainforests.

We won't survive without them. We won't survive without you.

PART TWO

Gifted Beginnings

We can't let our perceptions of giftedness dictate what we think of a child's gifts. Rather, we must learn to accept and meet these children where they are, so their talents and gifts will shine.

—Ginny Kochis

How to Explain Giftedness to Your Child

GAIL POST, PhD

What Should You Tell Your Child about Being Gifted?

Whether identified as gifted, referred for an evaluation, or placed in a gifted and talented program, children quickly form their own impressions. They may wonder if giftedness makes them different or smarter or weirder or better than the other kids. They may worry that they will become less popular or will be teased or bullied. *They might even want to stop being gifted altogether.*

Understanding Giftedness Is Not Easy

Understanding giftedness is complicated for adults. It is even more challenging for a six-, an eight-, or a ten-year-old child who is too young to fully grasp what giftedness means or place it in a context that makes sense. Gifted children already know they are different. They probably have heard both compliments and criticisms about their quirks, talents, and precocious behaviors. The "gifted" label can provide some validation for what they already know to be true, but it also might evoke confusion and anxiety.

Your Child Needs Your Help

Children need their parents to provide a framework for understanding what being gifted means. The following are some possible explanations you might offer your child.

"Gifted" Is Just a Word

"Gifted" doesn't mean that someone is better than anyone else. It was named a long time ago because people felt that it was a "gift" to be able to learn so easily. People might feel the same way about kids who run really fast or can slam dunk a basketball. You are fortunate to be able to learn so quickly. But it doesn't make you a better person. People are special for all kinds of wonderful reasons. Being gifted does not make someone any more special than the next person.

"Gifted" Is a Label Given to Kids Who Have Different Learning Needs

Everyone is different. Just like some people are taller or shorter than others, or more or less athletic, some people need a different approach in school to make learning more interesting. Everyone learns at a different pace, just like people grow taller at different rates. Some people need their teachers to teach a little more slowly, and others do best when they can move quickly through a subject. You seem to need teaching that lets you move quickly or spend a lot of time exploring a topic in depth.

You Were Found To Be Gifted Because of Some Tests You Took

We asked the school to give you these tests because you complained about being bored, or seemed distracted, or started to lose interest in subjects you used to like. We knew that if the testing labeled you as gifted, we could ask the school to give you more interesting work. We didn't care if you were gifted or not. We didn't care what score you got on any of the tests. The only reason for taking the tests was so the school could give you more choices and make school more interesting. Now that the school knows the results of your tests, they can find more interesting schoolwork that is better suited to what you need. (Note: It is never a good idea to tell young children their IQ score. Most children are not developmentally capable of understanding the meaning and significance of specific scores and could misinterpret the findings.)

Giftedness Is Something That Is a Part of You

Giftedness is just like your eye color or height. It doesn't come from how hard you work in school and will not go away if you slack off. It is always there and gives you some great choices to do some really creative/intensive/interesting/ (you fill in the blank) things. You cannot turn it on and off like a light switch. Being gifted affects how you see the world and think—not just how you perform in school. But, if you work hard, you can achieve a lot. If you don't, you will lose out on the opportunities your abilities have given you. Only *you* can make that choice.

You Are a Lot More than Your Giftedness

Even though being gifted is a part of who you are, it is not everything. There is so much more to you, and so much we love about you; your intelligence and talents are just one small piece. You have many great qualities and interests, and we are so happy that we get to know them all.

Giftedness Comes in All Shapes and Sizes

Some kids are really gifted with math. Some are great writers. Some are born leaders. Others paint up a storm. A few gifted children are good at many things; most are not. You have subjects in school that come really easily to you and interests that you love. We hope you continue to put a lot of energy into those things. But you still need to work hard in those areas that are not easy for you.

Gifted Children Sometimes Feel They Are Different from Other Kids

Even if you like how easy school is, it can be uncomfortable when you feel like you are different from a lot of the other kids in your class. It's normal to feel that way. We can help you to figure out what to say if other kids make comments about your interests. We also can help you find things you *do* have in common with some of the other kids or help you find outside activities that school does not offer. Being a kid can be hard for everyone—even for some of the other kids who look like they have it easy. Friendships may become easier to find when you get older, but we will help you get through whatever is hard for you right now.

Giftedness Is Not an Excuse

Being gifted does not mean school should be easy. We know that some of your classes may be too basic for you, which is why we are trying to find opportunities inside and outside of school that will challenge you. We don't expect you to be perfect but want you to try hard and put in your best effort. Success at anything takes hard work and discipline. Not everything you are going to do at school—or later in a job—is going to be interesting, so you have to learn to do the work even if you don't like it.

We Love You No Matter What

You don't have to be gifted or smart or talented or do well in school for us to love you. We love you for who you are and always will. You don't have to be perfect or prove anything or live up to your giftedness. You just need to figure out what interests you and let yourself delve into it. Of course, we would like you to put in effort in school—even when you don't like your classes. That's just life: Sometimes, you have to do things you don't want to do. But we don't love you any more or less because you are gifted. We love you because you are you!

Conclusion

The ideas discussed above are just a few suggestions for starting a conversation with your gifted child. You will need to modify them to suit your child's and your family's beliefs and values. What is most important, though, is conveying that you will help your child navigate their journey through giftedness and that ability and achievements play no role in your love for your child.

Most Gifted Children Have Never Been Studied

KATHLEEN HUMBLE

Can teachers spot gifted children?

How you answer that question is probably based on what you think gifted means. I have heard everything from "Of course they can!" to "Of course they can't!" So, how good are teachers at identifying gifted students? David Card and Laura Giuliano set out to find answers in the Broward County, Florida, public school system.[1]

The Broward County experiments were conducted to test whether teachers could spot gifted children. And, much like those in the *MythBusters*, they resulted in some unexpected outcomes.

What Were the Findings?

When a teacher chose a child for the gifted program, they had a 50% chance of getting it right (half of the kids they picked had a high IQ), which, even with the different definitions of giftedness (top 10% or top 2%), isn't bad. But the next bit is the kicker.

The researchers also tested all the kids the teachers didn't choose, and those results showed that teachers in Broward County only found 40% of gifted children, or 4 in every 10.[2]

Who was left out?

- ✧ Black kids
- ✧ poor kids
- ✧ disabled kids
- ✧ kids whose first language isn't English

This point is worth emphasizing: *When teachers looked at these kids, they saw disadvantage, not potential. And these disadvantaged kids were never chosen for gifted programs.*

This is why the Broward County experiments are so important: Almost none of the research on giftedness—beginning with the very first study by Terman—starts with an IQ test of an entire population. It starts with teachers picking out who to test.

That means that almost every test out there on giftedness and how "awesome" it is starts with eliminating the majority of children who are disadvantaged: they're poor, they're a member of a minority group, they don't speak the same language as their teachers, or they're disabled.

What happens when you gather a group of kids to test and exclude anyone who may not do well? Wow! They perform above average! Big surprise.

Giftedness Is Stressful

So, what about the kids who never make it into these studies? Do gifted kids just breeze through everything? Will they have no problems adapting to bad environments for their learning needs? Do they just succeed no matter what?

And what about the actual lived experience of parents of gifted kids? Is it all smooth sailing? Natalie Rimlinger, at The Australian National University, studied this and found the actual experience of raising a gifted child—with or without disabilities—was similar in stress level to that of raising a disabled child who is not gifted.[3] This drives home an important point: *Difference of ability doesn't cause stress. Lack of help and support for different abilities is what causes anxiety.*

If this sounds a lot like The Social Model of Disability, you're right.[4] In my opinion, this is evidence that looking at disability as a lack rather than a difference is fundamentally wrong. *It is the way we organize and cater for different needs that is the problem, not the different needs themselves.*

When children are in an environment that makes learning difficult, it's stressful, and they and their families suffer. It sucks when you're different and no one helps you.

Are we missing a bigger picture here? Is giftedness always an advantage? And how does it interact with other types of disadvantage?[5] We are largely still in the dark. By eliminating populations from studies, researchers (perhaps unintentionally) have skewed their results. And, from the little data we have, it looks like giftedness may be far more stressful, be less of an advantage, and have a lot more in common with disabilities than we previously thought.

I personally believe that many "truths" in educational norms aren't as solid as people think. And this mismatch between stereotype and reality causes much stress for families caught in the middle.

Where Does This Leave Us?

We just don't know what we don't know. There is a massive hole in the research. So, what about all the current studies? It's not that they're wrong; it's just that they may be more limited than we previously thought. Hence, our knowledge of gifted children is also lacking, primarily as a result of those who have been studied. One thing we can say for sure is that white, middle-class boys with educated parents do better if they're also identified as gifted.[6]

As for the rest? It looks as though there may be some progress being made. With the publication of the paper "A Culturally Responsive Equity-Based Bill of Rights for Gifted Students of Color," there has finally been some focus on this much neglected area.[7]

This has spurred work looking at Black gifted rural students, teacher equity training with a focus on giftedness, and where the barriers exist for gifted kids from minority backgrounds being included in gifted programs.[8,9,10] And this is only the beginning.

What is to come next? I certainly don't know. But I'd bet a solid dollar that much of it is going to "upset the apple cart." And that can't happen soon enough.

Five Reasons Gifted Children Aren't Motivated and Five Ways to Help

GINNY KOCHIS

K ate loved writing, and she was good at it too. Stories would flow from her fingertips like water, intricate plots and sophisticated characters rising from the depths. But Kate was in my survey course—a standard, high school English class. We were reading and analyzing literature, not writing it, and Kate was wholly uninterested.

I worked all year to reach her, but by April, I'd all but given up. There had been after-school sessions, parent-teacher conferences, and multiple opportunities to turn in late work.

The girl who should have been my strongest student was barely scraping by with a C. That is, until we got to poetry, and Kate's heavy form grew wings.

Kate had a habit of drawing dragons. They lounged on her binders, danced across class notes, and lurked atop homework like cats bathing in the sun. The day we did Photograffiti, Kate finally had license to be herself. Rather than struggle to analyze a staid piece of literature, Kate filled every inch of her guitar case with wings, scales, tales, and words. Her classmates and I gathered around, transfixed.

All the beauty and wisdom she'd held back that year poured out onto that plastic surface.

Kate was a girl transformed, and I was a teacher changed.

Gifted Stereotypes

Prior to Kate's appearance in my classroom, I had a stereotypical perception of what it meant to be gifted. I had classrooms full of gifted students, I thought: hard-working achievers who were eager to succeed.

36

I thought the gifted kids were the ones who never missed an assignment, who never struggled with concepts or tasks. They were supposed to be the perfect students. Smart kids who struggled were just lazy.

Fortunately, Kate appeared in my classroom a few years before my own poppies were born. I live in a house with three absent-minded professors: their rooms are a mess, their chores are undone, and their assignments for our homeschool co-op are largely ignored. Thanks to Kate's ability to open my eyes, I've discovered lackluster motivation and incomplete follow through aren't symptoms of poor behavior or attitude. What follows are five reasons your gifted child isn't motivated and five ways to help.

The Struggle: Perfectionism

For many gifted children, the fear of failure is stultifying. Rather than risk doing a task incorrectly, some children will eschew it altogether. My six-year-old is like this, and it's led to many a frustrating conflict. I know she's more than capable; she's convinced it won't be right.

The Solution: Perseverance

Carol Dweck's growth mindset has taken off like gangbusters, and it's easy to see why.[11] Her theory espouses that mistakes move us forward, that struggle and challenge are pathways to success. To help your child develop a spirit of perseverance, seek out examples of mistakes that turned out well. Read about historical figures who persevered in spite of great odds. Discuss favorite characters from books or movies whose missteps are a springboard for success. Recognizing the power in failure can go a long way toward liberation from the chains of perfection.

The Struggle: Temperament

Hippocrates had his own version of the Myers–Briggs Type Indicator personality inventory.[12] His four temperament theory referred to four personality types that can dictate a person's passions and behaviors. I have three of the four: sanguine (happy-go-lucky), choleric (headstrong and independent), and melancholic (sensitive and analytical). The fourth personality type, the phlegmatic, prefers to go with the flow and avoid conflict as much as possible.[13]

It's easy to see why different temperaments might struggle with motivation and completion of tasks. Sanguines won't be interested in activities that aren't enjoyable; cholerics will chafe at being told what to do. Melancholics might worry about doing something wrong, while phlegmatics get caught in the inertia of habit.

The Solution: Ownership

Children are more invested in tasks they choose. Ask your child how they want to help around the house or which activities excite them. In my house, my six-year-old loves to clean the sink; her older sister likes to cook. Those tasks fall to them, not me, and they're much more likely to do them because they're something to enjoy.

The great caveat to this is the spectrum of real life. Our kids must learn to accept and follow through on tasks they find uninspiring. But I find that starting with jobs they do like builds a healthy respect for the value of work. As they get older, they are better able to recognize the benefit of more distasteful efforts.

The Struggle: Intense Focus

My oldest child has always exhibited a strong capacity for concentration. As a toddler, she sat at the table for hours, occupying herself with Play-Doh, crayons, and the occasional audiobook. While this sort of attention has its advantages, it has definite downsides too: getting dressed isn't nearly as fascinating as the social habits of Komodo dragons, hair brushing is underrated when there are LEGO biomes to build, and messy rooms require substantially less attention than polluted watersheds and creeks. Just getting my child to brush her teeth in the morning is a struggle, especially when she's fixated on a certain topic.

The Solution: Clear, Visual Directions

With all the information processing that takes place in a gifted brain, a laundry list of tasks and expectations isn't going to sink in. To avoid overload and avoidance, offer clear, specific directions one at a time, perhaps in a visual format.

The Struggle: Asynchronous Development

With their capacity for deep understanding and their precocious personalities, gifted kids can seem a lot older than they are. But, where some aspects of their development leap forward in giant bounds, other aspects lag conspicuously behind. My fourth grader read *The Hobbit* in kindergarten, but she still hasn't figured out how to tie her own shoes. Sometimes, the easiest tasks seem insurmountable when asynchronous development comes into play.[14]

The Solution: Practice

Educational expert Harry Wong encourages first-year teachers to practice classroom procedures during the first few days of school.[15] Applying this concept in a home environment seems off-putting at first, but when you consider the reality of asynchronous development, helping a child practice new behaviors makes a lot of sense. Break down the steps involved in a task and take time teaching your child how to complete them. Even something as simple as packing a bookbag is worth practicing, especially if organizational skills aren't up to par.

The Struggle: Twice Exceptionality

Many gifted kids are twice exceptional (2e). Their abilities come hand in hand with a developmental or learning disability such as an autism spectrum disorder, ADHD, or dyslexia. Not only do these challenges inhibit a child's academic performance, they also have a tendency to impact executive functioning.

The Solution: Coping Mechanisms

If you're raising a 2e child, you probably already have some coping mechanisms in place. For my sensory kids, these include a heavy dose of physical exercise. The exertion helps my children order themselves and find their place in space. You may also be able to apply some of the same techniques used in your child's academic environment to their home life, and vice versa. Try experimenting with what works in one setting until you find something that works in another.

The Takeaway

I'm not proud of the length of time it took me to recognize what was going on with Kate. When I think about how much grief I could have saved her, my heart skips a few heavy beats. Rather than continue to force an incompatible strategy on a brilliant mind, I should have identified her challenges and adapted to them accordingly. My preconceived ideas kept me from recognizing the value in her inherent skills.

We can't let our perceptions of giftedness dictate what we think of a child's gifts. Rather, we must learn to accept and meet these children where they are, so their talents and gifts will shine.

Your Messy Kid Could Be a Perfectionist

HEATHER PLEIER

Perfectionism, like so many things, doesn't always look the way we expect it to.

For some kids, perfectionism looks like someone spending hours and hours laboring over draft after draft, making sure everything is just exactly so. But, for others, especially those who deal with executive function difficulties, it may look exactly the opposite.

It may look like scribbling, because they know no matter how hard they try, they won't get it completely within the lines, so it's easier to not try in the first place than to spend time and effort only to be disappointed.

It may look like tearing a tiny rip in a book accidentally and then going on to rip the entire page because they don't know how to handle the emotion of seeing their precious book damaged.

It may look like refusal to participate, whether in a creative activity or a game, because of fear of failure or mistakes.

It may look like spending way too much time on a specific detail and then not having time for the rest of the project, therefore sabotaging the entire thing in the process and making it look like they gave up when, in fact, they just ran out of time.

It may look like using too much water in a watercolor, making a small tear in the paper and then stopping painting to instead focus on enlarging that hole until the picture is unsalvageable.

Perfectionism is a dangerous beast because the intent—doing something well—is a trait to be admired. We praise attention to detail. We praise careful execution. When we fail to recognize the motivation behind our kids' (or our own) struggles, we approach their (or our) challenges with the wrong attitude.

Perfectionism Is a Mindset, Not a Result

Sometimes, we look at someone's sloppy work and think they couldn't possibly be a perfectionist, when, in fact, it's their perfectionism that may be preventing them from exerting themselves because they know, no matter how hard they try, they won't reach the ideal standard they've set in their minds. It's this thought process that may be causing them to destroy their work because it doesn't match their self-imposed expectations and they can't handle the frustration of not measuring up.

When We Recognize Their Self-Imposed Expectations, We Stop Applying External Pressure

Ceasing to add external pressure is one of the most valuable gifts we can give the perfectionists in our lives. When they're already putting tremendous pressure on themselves and we heap more on top, we stop being an encouragement and become a burden. We stop building them up and add to their already intense anxiety and stress. We, instead, need to help our perfectionists recognize that

✧ mistakes are part of life

✧ failure is normal

✧ the only way to improve is to work through the messy phases of trial and error

So, how do we do that?

✧ We point out (and normalize) our own mistakes. I even have an "everybody makes mistakes" song that I made up and sing— frequently—when things happen. It creates an atmosphere of acceptance and emphasizes that everyone, parents included, has off days and moments. Daniel Tiger has a song too: "It's okay to make mistakes/ try to fix them and learn from them too."[16] I love Daniel Tiger.

✧ We offer them space to be imperfect and not feel as if they have to measure up to society's expectations when it's not really necessary. My kids' clothes don't always match. They often wear mismatched socks or colors that clash. They turn in work at various venues that isn't perfect, but it's authentic. It's them. And they're owning it.

◇ We make sure that our relationships with them and others, especially family members, are unconditional, not based on external behavior or other measures.

◇ We provide lots of resources (books, biographies, mentors, etc.) that normalize other people's mistakes and imperfections so they know they're not alone.

◇ We give them room to be kids and celebrate that they don't have to be as good as, as smart as, as "whatever" as the kid next door in order to have value.

◇ We teach them ways to cope when they're frustrated or overwhelmed in a situation and how to verbalize what they're feeling, and we let them know that they are loved for who they are, no matter what.

In the end, what matters is that our kids are learning who they are, what they're passionate about, and how to express themselves. A particularly messy coloring page will not matter 10 years down the road, but the way we respond to that unmet expectation and foster our children's potential does matter. Our relationships matter, their trust in us matters, and their opinions of themselves and their abilities matter.

We have a choice, every time we encounter these big emotions and frustrations, either to choose empathy and connection or to focus on the product rather than the child. Yes, sometimes, we will ask for a redo. We aren't walking away from all expectations or standards, but we will put those in perspective and nurture the gifts we've been given.

The Tyranny of Pathologizing Our Kids

HEATHER BOORMAN

When did it happen? When did the energetic child become the child with hyperactivity? The opinionated child become the oppositional child? The stubborn child become the defiant child? The daydreaming child start having attention deficits? When did we start pathologizing our kids?

I guess, in many ways, it doesn't entirely matter how we got here, as long as we acknowledge that we are indeed here. We have become deficit focused. We look at our kids' behaviors and try to "fix them," so we slap a diagnosis on, begin behavior modification programs, shove medications at them, and call it a day. Sure, as a therapist, I fully know and accept that there are times when those diagnoses are needed and accurate. I also know that many children are walking around being treated for disorders they do not, in actuality, have. I've seen kids on medications they don't need. I've seen kids pigeonholed based on diagnoses that merely describe symptomatic behavior rather than identify genuine disorders.

Oppositional defiant disorder (ODD), for example. I'm going to be bold here and straight out say that I do not believe this to be a genuine disorder. I have yet to encounter a child diagnosed with ODD whose behaviors weren't explainable by an underlying situation or alternate mental health concern. Sure, they may defy authority, but usually that's because they are anxious, or insecure, or traumatized, or sensorily overloaded, or incapable of doing the task requested of them.

Attention-deficit/hyperactivity disorder (ADHD) is another example. I will not be so black and white with this one, as I think there's a case to be made in support of this disorder's existence and a case to be made that this disorder is actually something else. Either way, the one thing I do know for sure about ADHD is that it continues to be criminally overdiagnosed and overmedicated. ADHD is meant to be a diagnosis of last resort—a condition to be diagnosed only after all other possibilities have been ruled out. And, yet, it is often the

43

first thing adults look to when they see a child who is a little bouncier than typical or a little more distractible than their age peers.

Why should this matter? Because when we slap on these diagnoses, and others, without careful differentiation, time, and observation, we end up missing the point. We end up failing our kids. Behavior is not a disorder. Behavior is communication. Instead of listening to and decoding the messages our kids are sending us, we end up treating symptoms. And, when that only works for a short time, we end up treating the symptoms more fiercely. All the while, the poor kid hasn't had their real needs met in the slightest.

But, really, it goes beyond that. Not only have these children not had their needs met, but they've been told there's something about them that needs fixing and that's wrong. Kids whose behaviors would be expected when the circumstances are understood feel shamed for these very behaviors.

Our kids on the fringes of typicality are particularly vulnerable. The child whose sensory processing has a few glitches attempts to gain control of their environment in order to minimize the assault against their brain. They're diagnosed with ODD, get labeled the bad kid, and continue to appear defiant because their sensory issues haven't been addressed, so they need to rely on the only coping skill they know. The profoundly gifted child whom everyone understands to be "smart" but also experiences the world with such intensity that their body simply can't sit still gets diagnosed with ADHD and put on medications that directly impact their brain chemistry. Their cognitive abilities may drop, they may become more irritable, and their innate spark silently dims.

To be clear, I have no problem with medications when medications are actually needed. I am an advocate for acknowledging real mental health issues and helping families find the support and treatment they need. I think diagnoses can be helpful and informative.

I do have a problem with misunderstanding and misdiagnosing our most vulnerable. I have a problem with pathologizing typical behaviors. I have a problem with jumping to the quick answer with a rapid treatment instead of taking the time to listen to what the child is trying to communicate regarding what's going on under the surface. I have a problem with blaming the child instead of looking to the environment to see how their needs aren't being met.

Let's stop pathologizing our kids. Let's learn more about the different needs of our atypically developing kids and find new ways to meet those needs. Let's listen to the behaviors instead of trying to quickly get rid of them. Let's actually give our kids what they need.

Understanding Extreme Gifted Boy Behavior

TERESA CURRIVAN

In my world of working with gifted homeschoolers and twice-exceptional children in gifted schools, and of being a mother to one, I am seeing a pattern among some of the boys. It's a feedback loop that seems to start in school but, when strengthened, can seep into relationships with both parents and educators. Let me explain.

The boy has a behavior that is understandably misunderstood. It is a behavior that scares us. It can look like bullying or violence, biting sarcasm, or even just a little meanness. The adults react (or overreact) and the child, in turn, reacts to the adults, which can cause these behaviors to grow stronger and manifest in more extreme ways. As can be expected, the adult's reactions then become stronger as well. Because the boy feels that no one has faith in his goodness anymore, eventually, he begins to internalize the adults' perceptions of him and sees himself as a "bad kid." Even when the adults are not saying "You're a bad kid," or even when they are saying the opposite, the child knows by their reactions how he's being perceived. He feels that he is essentially bad. If the feedback loop continues, he may fall into a self-fulfilling prophecy and, by high school age, perceive himself as a hopeless case. He throws in the towel and begins not to care.

But let's rewind and take a look at a boy who is just beginning this pattern. Mathew, a first grader in a typical public school, possesses high degrees of emotional, psychomotor, and intellectual overexcitabilities (OEs).[17] His behaviors related to these OEs are beginning to show up in obvious ways.

Mathew's high sensitivity shows up in ways that are interpreted in reverse—as being low in sensitivity and uncaring. In fact, he cares very much how he is perceived, especially how he is seen by his parents as well as by his peers and the adults whom he admires. But he hides this through silly behavior and sometimes anger when his parents become upset at him. In addition, he has a certain rigidity over how people should behave. He has a strong sense of social justice, and when he sees anyone treated unfairly, especially by adults, his feelings of anger are quite overwhelming. When combined with his yet-to-be-developed ability to see a problem from another's perspective, his behavior can lead to great misunderstandings about his intentions.

In one incident, when a boy in Mathew's class got in trouble for hitting another boy and faced expulsion, Mathew became very upset. According to Mathew, the child who was hit had said something extremely hurtful to the boy who hit him. In Mathew's eyes, the teachers overreacted to the incident, shaming the boy who did the hitting. Parents were brought in and other children were asked not to interact with this boy. Mathew felt both children were in the wrong; in fact, Mathew later interviewed the boys involved and both admitted as much.

Mathew's mother tried to explain that physically hurting someone at school has to be taken seriously by the staff—it's "just the way it is, especially in the public school system." This made Mathew angrier. That an arbitrary rule would override a social justice issue was his hot button. He didn't have the emotional space to step back and see the problem as a larger issue, as most adults reading this probably can.

His reaction was strong, and mostly in his body, as though he needed to fight someone. He said he wanted to fight the school. His mother tried to explain how things are done and that he wouldn't be solving anything were he to take action in anger. In response, he cited various tyrannical governments and asked what the difference was between them and his school. (Yes, this is first grade, but maybe you know the type.)

At one point, one of his friends reported that Mathew had talked of blowing up the school. When his mother asked Mathew about the people who would be hurt, he replied that he would make sure no one was hurt. Mathew had never carried out a plan such as this, and his mother was certain that his words were from his imaginary realm—just his way of expressing frustration. In our current atmosphere of fear of security in our schools, Mathew's words understandably triggered alarm from adults, which made him respond even more strongly. From the outside, Mathew's behavior might be labeled as sociopathic by some, but in this case, it is his OEs that need to be understood and tempered by the adults. Over time, this type of behavior could develop into defiance if left unchecked. This depends, in part, on how the adults respond to the behavior and of course, in part, on the individual boy.

After speaking with me and understanding how Mathew's OEs impact his ability to respond to situations such as this, Mathew's mother wasn't sure she could help the school understand where Mathew's rebelliousness was coming from. This was a busy public school, with bigger problems to deal with.

Knowing that Mathew's mother and the boy's teacher had a good relationship and that Mathew had found this teacher's daily mindfulness exercises relaxing, I suggested they have a meeting. There, Mathew's mother explained her son's motivation behind the threat and succeeded in getting his teacher to understand the depth of Mathew's feelings around the perceived injustice to his classmate.

The teacher was able to have a heart-to-heart discussion with Mathew from which things shifted for the boy. While he continues to be an advocate for social justice, he has dropped his fantasy of blowing up the school. Mathew's mother told me that his teacher had a lesson plan on Martin Luther King Jr. and explained how he had been a fierce advocate for social justice, "like Mathew is."

While this is likely to be an ongoing theme in Mathew's life, I truly believe that his teacher, in her mindful and nonreactive way, was instrumental in helping him through one major level of understanding, not only by what she said but by how she handled and responded to him. It took great empathy and skill for her to accept some responsibility in understanding the cause of Mathew's stress and to change *her* reactivity. My hope is that Mathew can internalize his teacher's ability to react thoughtfully when under stress.

In this way, a mindful adult can help interrupt the feedback loop that many of our boys get into, in which their reactions become stronger and more defensive as they feel the authority figure's negative reaction to them. This is a common conundrum for this type of intensity. Mathew is just one example of the many boys who possess these emotional, physical, and intellectual OEs. Knowing the complexity of each child's unique OEs and taking the time to understand the situations where they seem unable to regulate themselves in a mindful way will ultimately help them to find healthy solutions for themselves, in turn creating adults who can do the same. And, wow, wouldn't that help create the world we want?

The Heartbreak of Angry Gifted Kids

GINNY KOCHIS

Angry children don't rage for anger's sake. Rather, their behavior is a symptom of a deeper issue. What follows is a close look at the anatomy of angry gifted children and suggestions for helping them cope.

I have angry kids. They are also brilliant, sensitive, loving, and empathetic, but those things don't garner the attention of authority figures in a school or enrichment class.

What does?

- ✧ Hitting the art teacher
- ✧ Telling a fellow student to "bug off, you black-hearted maggot"
- ✧ Responding to direction with "you can't force me to do anything"
- ✧ Breaking a glass figurine by throwing it across the room

Yep. Nothing makes you question your parenting ability (read: sanity) more than a child who's the perpetrator in an incident report. Or a child who makes you flinch. Or a child who causes your fingers to hover over the dial pad of your smartphone.

But I've learned something over my years of parenting—the rage is never anger for anger's sake. Instead, it's the first line of defense for a more deep-seated emotion. Punishment doesn't do anything. It's understanding and forgiveness that do.

Anatomy of an Angry Gifted Child

The word "gifted" is a misnomer. Giftedness isn't a gift so much as it is a difference, a biological variation from the norm. Brain scans of gifted individuals have revealed startling information: Neural pathways (or "hubs," as scientists refer to them) tend to be denser in individuals with higher IQ levels.

48

The denser the neural hub, the more efficient the processing of information: Such scans are physical evidence of a gifted person's increased processing speed.[18]

But the brain is a complex organ, and even one small deviation can have a cascading effect. I often try to explain it in terms of planting a vegetable garden: If I only have so much acreage, I'm going to watch my spacing, right?

What happens, though, if I have a whole bunch of carrots and I've put them among broccoli seedlings? When my plants start growing, one of those two is going to crowd the other. I might end up with a beautiful crop of carrots amid struggling shoots of broccoli. Now, in this particular garden of mine, I know the broccoli will grow. But it will be slower, more deliberate than its bold orange counterpart.

This is how I look at my gifted children's brain development. They have a whole heck of a lot of carrots growing like gangbusters. The broccoli? It's in there, but there are signs it's not doing as much—yet. I realize it's an unscientific analogy, but the point I'm trying to make here is that a gifted child's brain grows differently and this difference in growth is going to have lasting developmental effects.

Start with asynchronous development.[19] Yes, this really is a thing. While a gifted child's brain erupts in leaps and bounds in some areas, other areas follow an average or below average progression. You might have an 11-year-old who academically is ready for high school work but socially and emotionally is two to three years below grade level.

Then, consider the likelihood of overexcitabilities.[20] Gifted children think, feel, and react more deeply to every sense and situation: Sounds are louder, smells are stronger, and emotional reactions can be off the charts. Together, asynchronous development and overexcitabilities have a major impact on emotional regulation. It is difficult for a child to navigate big feelings under the best of circumstances. Imagine trying to do so while under direct sensory and emotional assault.

Enter the anger. Want to have your heart broken? Take a close look at an angry gifted kid. Angry kids don't want to be angry. They don't want to lash out, hurt feelings, or be rude. In my children's experience, it's a symptom of a larger problem. They aren't hateful, spiteful, or the least bit vindictive. They're actually caught in the throes of an emotional trigger and unable to manage the feelings they're experiencing.

Common Emotional Triggers for Angry Gifted Kids

Anxiety

Anxiety and anger are strange bedfellows because people often assume they exist in opposition. I know I did, which meant getting to the bottom of my daughter's struggles took much longer. We'd had a host of broken toys and all-out screaming matches before I finally got it.

The connection between anger and anxiety lies in the fight or flight response. Most people tend to freeze in the face of great anxiety. In gifted kids, the emotion is frequently stifled until the child finally erupts.

Perfectionism

The desire for perfection is killer. Case in point: On one occasion, a dance teacher demanded my eldest leave the classroom. Turns out the precipitating incident was actually related to a missed audition. My daughter was berating herself inwardly; the dance teacher simply asked her to get up off the floor.

We've spent a lot of time talking about self-advocacy, but my poor child was immersed in a really bad case of self-deprecation. How was she supposed to tell an adult her most inward, private failings? She lashed out rather than asking for a moment to collect herself, and just like that, she was out the door.

Introspection

Gifted kids know they are different. They know they stand out, and they know people make assumptions. Can you imagine being 10 years old and telling a new friend what you learned about the Hadron Collider?

That loneliness takes time to sort out.

Because children are unique and unrepeatable, there are more triggers than those listed above. You may find your child struggles with one or more of the following:

- ✧ a heightened sense of justice—they can feel overwhelming frustration when they sense someone has been wronged
- ✧ a great degree of empathy—some soak up tension like a sponge
- ✧ impatience—it is difficult to keep your cool when the rest of the world can't keep up

Coping Skills

A child's angry outburst is a cry for help. As parents, we're responsible for passing on the coping skills that will help our children thrive:

- ✧ Tell your child the realities about perfectionism. Help them see perfection as perseverance, as becoming the person they're created to be.
- ✧ Teach and model emotional awareness. Talk through your own patterns of escalation and how you work to disarm yourself.

✧ Set firm limits. Use phrases such as "I know you are angry right now, and it's okay to be angry but (hitting, kicking, throwing, etc.) isn't an acceptable response."

✧ Accentuate the positive. Find and celebrate the moments your child exhibits positive emotional regulation.

✧ Teach empathy. Model empathetic behavior, especially when it comes to your child's emotions.

✧ Offer an arsenal of calming tools (movement, journaling, music, etc.).

✧ Provide opportunities for choice and ownership. Help your child make amends for things said and done in anger and teach them to view it as a positive step.

✧ Work on a growth mindset to ease the fear of failure.[21]

✧ Front-load the reality of a situation to avoid meltdowns over unmet expectations.

✧ Talk to the adults (coaches, teachers, etc.) who are involved in your kids' lives. Encourage your children to do the same.

I have angry children. I also have children who are loving, empathetic, and brave.

As their mother, it's my job to respect those big emotions. An angry child's outburst is a symptom, not an issue in and of itself.

22 Lines a Gifted Child Hates to Hear

LISA SWABODA

Over the years, I've heard these lines often, but only now do I understand what they really mean. Only now do I understand why they stung so much. Maybe to some kids they were innocuous, or only said in a matter-of-fact way that was easily accepted; but, to me, they were stifling, a "Road Closed" sign, a way to cut me off and cut me down. Have you had similar frustrations?

"You ask too many questions."

"Because you're too young."

And my personal all-time *very* worst: "Because I said so."

These lines always implied that I was too young, was not knowledgeable enough (hence, the old conundrum: *Experience—How do you get it without getting it?*), or that someone else knew what was best for me.

School brought lines like these

✧ "The *why* isn't important." (This one's particularly outrageous to me.)

✧ "Follow these directions—exactly."

✧ "Memorize this."

✧ "Stop dreaming."

✧ "Use only these colors." (Uh, why?)

✧ "There's no room for creativity today." (Kill me now.)

Time limitations always seemed to bring out the worst

✧ "We don't have time for questions." (Really?!)

✧ "You've been working on that long enough." (One of the best reasons to homeschool a gifted child.)

✧ "Put that away; it's time to…"

Who doesn't wish to explain the reasoning behind a choice when others see it as incorrect?

✧ "Stop explaining."

✧ "Why are you always analyzing everything?" (This, I discovered, was actually a rhetorical question.)

✧ "No explanation needed." (I followed up this one with my question, "But is it OK if I give one?")

✧ "Why do you always have to be right?" (I often heard this when I was in opposition to an answer, even while ready with my evidence. I never did but always wanted to ask, "Why do you?" I later discovered this was also a rhetorical question. I wonder: Do *all* gifted children come to understand the concept of a rhetorical question later in life?)

When different means wrong

✧ "Yours should look like mine."

✧ "I'll show you the *right* way to do it."

✧ "There's only *one* correct answer." (Argh!)

Then, there were the intended criticisms that I always took as compliments

✧ "You're always thinking." (LOL!)

✧ "You read too much."

✧ "This is unrealistic." (So is your world to me.)

It's pretty clear that these lines aren't going away anytime soon, but at least maybe you can share them with your favorite gifted kid and let them know that there are other people out there who really *do* understand.

The Awesome Weirdness of Gifted Kids

JEN MERRILL

Gifted kids be weird, yo.

If you have one, or have spent any time around one, or teach one, you know this. They are the quirkiest, funniest, weirdest creatures around. And, if you can step away from the challenging behaviors and parental angst, they're awesome.

It's taken me a long time to get to this point, to appreciate the weird in gifted. Yes, I've always tried to laugh at it, or at the very least poke fun at it, but appreciate it? Not an easy thing to do, especially when you're in the thick of one crisis after another trying to deal with it. How are you supposed to appreciate your kids' quirks and humor when you're simultaneously trying to put out the fires those quirks are fanning? Not a job for the faint of heart, and surely not one any of us applied for. Yet, here we are. Might as well make some s'mores over those flames.

Here is just a small sample of the tidbits I've laughed at over the years. Names have been withheld to protect the innocent.

Do black holes ever close?

Um. I have degrees in music and advanced degrees in parenting that I earned on the job. Inevitably, you asked this before I had coffee or after I had wine. Either way, I have no answer for you because the question itself broke my brain. Let's go with, "Maybe, but I reserve the right to change my mind when scientists come forth with further information. In the meantime, please go research that yourself."

Heck, MacGyver can make a stretcher with a couple paper clips and duct tape!

Yes, yes he can. That still doesn't mean I'm giving you the zip ties, ball bearings, 4 feet of metal conduit, and rubber chicken you requested. And hell

54

to the no on the liquid nitrogen, stevia plant, and rare earth magnets. What are you doing in the basement?

Guy walks into a bar. It was a metal bar. He got hurt.

You're still working on your jokes. Not bad for a first try, but keep honing your craft. Also, keep your day job.

The future will come. It always does.

When parenting goes meta on you. Thanks, child, needed the reminder. Your future is also speeding up on you and you'll (1) be starving at school tomorrow if you don't get going on making a lunch or (2) be living in the basement if you don't acknowledge that college is heading this direction.

The only thing I hate about getting older is the responsibilities.

I let said child live. I also laughed until I fell to the ground and could not breathe. Child was not amused. I cannot wait until I can share this tidbit with this child when he is older and has real responsibilities. I saved the name, date, and time of when he popped out this comment, and I may just needle that sucker into a cross-stitch and keep it on hand for proper presentation. I'm thinking college graduation. Been almost three years and I still laugh and laugh and laugh.

Why can't I take in air through the atmosphere? My head hurts!

Son in question had just had two teeth removed and was still woozy from the laughing gas. This particular child is a freaking laugh riot under anesthesia; we still laugh about the time he was coming to and damned near stuck a popsicle in his eye.

It always comes down to the last level of logic for me.

Aaaand—I have nothing for this. Of course it does, dear son. Because you are wired the way you are, of course it comes down to the last level of logic. You needed to wring every last drop of logic out of all the previous levels. However, I've discovered that you always seem to find one last level, so your levels of logic are a lot more like a bottomless pit—or a "Highway to Hell"—for me. You're exhausting.

Why does my saliva not bounce around in my mouth when I'm bouncing on this ball?

For the same reason a hippopotamus wears a G-string on National Donut Day, kiddo.

What's wrong with me and my binaries?

What do your binaries have to do with anything? Did I miss a memo? Where are they? Are they inflamed? Do you need to see a doctor or an IT specialist? Are they contagious? I'd hate to be quarantined because of binaries. Do they need watering? My god, what happens if we feed them after midnight?

Flavor doesn't have copy and paste, MOM!

Dammit I wish I could remember the context here. I want to say it had something to do with chewing gum, but I just don't know. But you're right, buddy, flavor doesn't have copy and paste. If it did, I'd be throwing ⌘-c and ⌘-p around with wild abandon. Bananas that could taste like chocolate peanut butter ice cream instead of hot glue? Cauliflower with the flavor of ripe cherries instead of spicy funk? Zucchini that … never mind, nothing can improve zucchini. Devil's veggie. A hot pox on that vegetable.

I have a hurt-bump.

I do too, my loves. My head, it's pounding with the effort of understanding half of what you guys say and know. You're far smarter than I, and I'm starting to think you know it. But, unlike most physical hurt-bumps, this one won't go away with application of ice and a few ibuprofen. It's a permanent parenting-gifted-kids hurt-bump. Thankfully, it doesn't hurt anymore, just gets tender from time to time. It's a hurt-bump I didn't expect to be given, but one I wear like a badge of honor.

PART THREE

Gifted Gets Schooled

I began to embrace your quirks, your passions, and your struggles. When other teachers spoke about your differences, I became your champion. I began to take delight in you—yes, even on those tough days. You were the reason I stayed in the classroom as long as I did. You were the spark that kept me going.

—Lisa Swaboda

Dear Gifted Child

LISA SWABODA

I know this comes as too little too late, but I still feel the need to apologize to you. I hope you can forgive me. I now realize how much I let you down. It's no excuse, but I can now admit that I did what I did because I wanted to fit in. I thought I'd found my place at the time. All I can offer is … I didn't know.

I didn't know that by asking you to redo work over and over due to careless mistakes that I was doing you a disservice. I thought I was helping you to think more (even though as a child I was frustrated the same way).

I didn't know that by asking you to work in a group without easing you into expectations and supporting you with social skills, I was increasing the pressure you already felt (even though as a child I felt the same).

I didn't know that by taking away your book when you finished your work so quickly, I was showing my lack of faith in your abilities (even though it happened to me often as a child).

I didn't know that those times you wanted to tell me all about your Pokémon cards, or airplanes, or horses that dismissing you so quickly meant you'd have no one to share your knowledge with at recess (even though my own cravings to have someone listen that way are buried deep inside).

I didn't know that being gifted meant truly being different. I thought you were spoiled, lucky, arrogant, and bossy at times. That's what many other teachers thought, so who was I to disagree (even though I've often been called the same).

I didn't know how alone you felt with your offbeat wit, divergent thinking, and need to be understood (even though I've often felt the same).

I didn't know … I was you.

I treated you often the way I'd always been treated—as if you were annoying.

I treated you often with frustration—because you didn't fit in and didn't make my life easier.

I treated you the same as the others—even though you were different.

For that, I am sorry.

Secretly at first, and then as I gained confidence and years in teaching, I began to buck the system. I realized I was never going to fit in the same way as others. I began to embrace your quirks, your passions, and your struggles. When other teachers spoke about your differences, I became your champion. I began to take delight in you—yes, even on those tough days. *You* were the reason I stayed in the classroom as long as I did. *You* were the spark that kept me going.

You, dear gifted child (identified and not), were always my favorite and now I finally understand why.

I loved you best so I would love myself.

Intelligence Denied: When Gifted Children's Abilities Are Ignored

GAIL POST, PhD

In his baccalaureate address at Brown University's 2016 commencement, Kevin Gover, director for the National Museum of the American Indian, described some of his early childhood experiences. Among other things, he noted that when he was a child, he *knew* that he was smart; but, as part Native American, he struggled to reconcile this self-awareness with negative portrayals of indigenous people as lacking in intelligence. He recalled, regretfully, how he attributed his own intelligence to the fact that his mother was white, so completely had he internalized the powerful racist messages of that era.[1]

What happens when gifted children know they are smart but society or schools tell them they are wrong? What happens when they sense they are different from their peers but no one tells them why?

Whether their abilities are blatantly dismissed because of cultural, racial, or gender stereotypes, or merely minimized due to ignorance about giftedness in the schools, gifted children historically have struggled to thrive under conditions that attempt to suppress them. Gifted children *know* they are different. They see how they grasp information more easily and learn more quickly than many of their peers. They sometimes become impatient with friends who don't get it. They often react to events with greater emotionality and sensitivity. They may not fit in and can feel lonely and estranged.

Without proper guidance, gifted children will flounder. Unless identified early, offered a challenging education tailored to their needs, and allowed to flourish in a setting with like-minded peers, gifted children not only often fail to reach their potential, they may never understand the exceptional abilities they possess.

Who are typically ignored?

The list of gifted children who are frequently ignored is long and typically includes children of color, the poor, English language learners,

61

those with disabilities, twice-exceptional learners, girls lacking in confidence, roughhousing boys who just want to play, those who are not verbally precocious, and those in impoverished schools or who reside in a state where gifted services are not legally required. Essentially, any child can be overlooked. And, in some situations, giftedness is minimized or ignored even when the schools recognize that a child is gifted.

When giftedness is denied, dismissed, or ignored, negative outcomes can occur.

They know they are different but cannot understand why. Gifted children may feel confused about their differences. They realize how easily they grasp ideas and information when compared with their peers but cannot put these differences in context. As a result, they are left to form their own conclusions about their giftedness. They may ascribe too much meaning to their abilities or refuse to grant them any credibility. They may deny their giftedness, discount it, minimize it, distort it, exaggerate it, compartmentalize it, or feel guilty about it.

They may think there is something wrong with them. Gifted children (and adults) are often highly sensitive and emotionally reactive and possess a heightened sense of fairness and justice. They are sometimes prone to overthinking, perfectionism, and existential worries as they ponder the meaning of life. Since they do not necessarily see their same-age peers struggling with these same concerns, they may view themselves as social misfits and outliers or flawed and emotionally unstable.

They become chronically bored in school and learn to disrespect the system. Gifted students whose abilities are ignored can become bored and may assume traditional learning environments are a waste of time. While some passively withdraw, others become vocal about their dissatisfaction and cause trouble for themselves and others at school. They may disparage teachers they view as inadequate and, ultimately, develop chronic distrust for those in positions of authority.

They fail to reach their potential, having missed out on challenge, stimulation, or effective training at critical points in their development. Gifted children who are never challenged and who coast through school do not have an opportunity to hone their skills through meaningful learning and practice. Many children are never even identified as gifted, as a result of ignorance about "what giftedness looks like," lack of universal screening, or racial/cultural/gender stereotypes, creating an *excellence gap* for minority students.[2,3] Some schools also maintain policies that prevent acceleration, ability grouping, or truly differentiated instruction. Gifted students are held back when forced to endure repetitive, rote assignments instead of being offered challenging learning options that would encourage their growth and development.

They assume that they never have to work hard. Gifted students who are never challenged and who easily receive good grades often become complacent. They assume academics should come easily to them and never develop the executive functioning or study skills necessary for later success. Receiving a low grade may come as a shock, and they may steer clear of any difficult future challenges rather than risk failure. Some become underachievers under the radar, acquiring good grades and even awards but never pushing themselves beyond their comfort zone.[4] Others may become selective consumers, choosing to excel only in subjects that are meaningful and to give up when a topic does not interest them.[5]

Obviously, not all unidentified or unchallenged gifted children develop problems. However, efforts to improve gifted identification and help gifted children to understand what it means to be gifted are essential. Identification not only informs an educational plan aimed at enhancing their development but can clear up confusion and misunderstanding about traits these children recognize but cannot quite name. And providing gifted services tailored to their academic needs is critical to their educational growth as well as their development of resilience in the face of challenging tasks. It also offers reassurance that the adults in charge truly understand and are making every attempt to help them thrive.

Underachievement According to Whom?

JEN MERRILL

Please, someone, tell me you also sometimes take the 30,000-foot view of humanity while lost in thought—stepping back from the day-to-day nonsense and inspecting humanity as though we're insects as viewed from a high-altitude jet. I do it most often when I'm driving alone, silence as my favorite music, wondering who we are and how we got here. I'll pick out an object and contemplate all the people and thoughts and knowledge that came together to create it. I'm writing at the library, and everywhere I look I see this. The signs indicating the different book locations were designed by one person, the font created by another, the paint made and chosen by others, printed and assembled by still others, hanging from wires someone entirely different designed and manufactured, bolted into rafters designed and painted and manufactured and installed by still others. It goes on and on. Even the smallest, most insignificant part to a larger entity has someone's touch on it.

As a species with opposable thumbs and enough gray matter to give us raging anxiety, we're amazing in that we have created nearly all we see and a whole lot we don't. We've built the humblest hut to the awe-inspiring International Space Station; handshake agreements to multinational accords. Nothing has come down from on high; we've done it all ourselves. We've designed systems of governing and ways to educate our young. High fives all around; we're awesome.

So, if we're so awesome…

My favorite thought experiment is, "The zombie apocalypse has occurred. Society as we know it is kaput. What does our educational system look like now?" (Go read *The Passage* by Justin Cronin. Yes, Book 1 is awesome, Book 2 irritated me, and I haven't read Book 3.⁶) I'm willing to bet that in such a situation we no longer care about standards and achievement. So, how about we take the 30,000-foot view now and skip the whole zombie apocalypse thing entirely? My zombie apocalypse plan is to throw myself to the ravenous

64

hordes so as to save my sons, and while it looks like I've been fattening up for the opportunity, I'd really like to avoid that at all costs. My brain and my hips are for me, thank you very much.

If we are so awesome as a species, to have created such things as the International Space Station, push-up bras, and Dippin' Dots ice cream snacks, surely we can recreate our educational system. If a student is described as an underachiever, please tell me—according to whom? What metric? We came up with those metrics and cutoffs; we can change them.

Underachievement is a label humans have come up with based on an educational system we created. Really, what is underachievement? Achieving below a random standard created by the very species that evaluates itself.

Soooo…

Does underachievement really exist then? How about we rethink this? Again, take the 30,000-foot view.

There is no underachievement. There is only how a person (young or old) contributes to society in the way they best can. That could be as a physician; that could be as a storyteller; that could be as a farmer; that could be as a comforting lap in which to land, to be loved, and to be accepted for who one is at their core. I am a huge proponent of technical education; I've seen the benefits firsthand. My son Andy attended our county's Tech Campus for two years as well as Skills USA Nationals for two years in a row—in the Computer Information Technology area. People look down on VoTech, but it's a vital educational option for so many of our students.

Underachievement is the result of an educational system hell-bent on ranking students coming through the schools. It's something we created, so it's something we can change. It doesn't have to be this way. I don't believe any student is an underachiever. I believe that if a student is labeled as an underachiever, it's the fault of the educational system, not the fault of the student. Every student achieves in their own way, as they are able, as best as they are supported.

My husband and I are achievers—overachievers in many ways. Schools would tell us that at least one of our sons is an underachiever. Taking the entire educational juggernaut out of the equation, I see us as individuals working with our strengths while managing our weaknesses the best we can. (Yes, overachievers have weaknesses; we just learn to hide them early.) We are all human, we are all contributing as we can, we are all worthy. While I believe in some labels, the underachievement label is not one of them.

I think we can do better. I hope someday we will do better. Underachievement is just a construct we created; it does not actually exist.

A Tunnel and the Light at the End of It

JULIE SCHNEIDER

My children are mere elementary schoolers, but we have come to the light at the end of a tunnel. It is among the first tunnels we've traversed as a family, and our accomplishment deserves a small celebration. This is the story of how a gifted child learned to read—"late."

The nursery was dim, lit only by the soft glow of a small table lamp. The heirloom rocking chair, one generations of Mama Schneiders had shared with their babies, supported me entirely. My infant son sat in my lap while I read to him. It was a nightly routine I began early because I, myself, am a reader. And I fully intended to introduce my son to the wonderful world of books.

A handful of board books were stacked nearby, and I had a habit of reading them in the same order. That evening, I thought I should let my son choose. So, after reading the first book, I set it down and picked up two more and asked, "Which one next?" My son grabbed the one that had historically been next. I was surprised and wondered if he had just aced his first quiz, choosing it because he recognized the pattern. We enjoyed the stories in turn before he fell asleep in my arms.

That first year as a mother was truly amazing. Like mothers do, I watched my son learn to roll over, crawl, and walk. I attended to his needs—responding when he cried, feeding him, and changing his diaper. I especially enjoyed celebrating his discoveries: the first time he watched a bird on the sidewalk in front of him jump into the air and fly away, the never-ending game of "drop" to watch how the spoon (or whatever) fell to the floor when he let go of it, the way he tried to grab water while it streamed from the faucet. He was intrigued by the way things work; I was intrigued by his learning, to what he gave his attention.

In fact, in those first 12 months, he discovered his first passion: machines. It started with a little red race car toy that he played with endlessly. He tossed it and watched it roll; he lay on his belly and gently pushed it back and forth while he gazed at the wheels.

Shortly thereafter, his interest grew to include working trucks (dump trucks, backhoe loaders, etc.) and (due to the ubiquity of Thomas the Tank Engine) trains. We watched videos, learned songs, and read books about trucks. On our bike rides around town—to the grocery store and playgrounds—we would stop and watch machines work at construction sites. He was obsessed.

If it were up to him, we would do nothing but enjoy trucks and working machines all day every day. And, while I indulged him (quite a bit in fact), I still chose to read fiction to him and I took him to play at a variety of places with different friends. Our repertoire remained broad because of it.

He was a quiet little guy. As a one-year-old, he said only three words—mama, papa, and yeah. He used sign language for please, thank you, more, help, and swing. But no one seemed worried about his intellect. He was lively and engaged with the world around him. (Arguably, too engaged—he spent an inordinate amount of time investigating why his rattle only sometimes made noise.) He could bring us items based on their name and description. He seemed to understand quantity. He learned to crawl and walk with his same-aged peers. We assumed it would all even out eventually—when he was ready, he would speak.

In the meantime, I learned to intuit his needs as we built a life together. We became regulars at the local playgrounds, library, grocery store, and children's museum. We made friends. We read books. It was a life rich with the typical features of early childhood development (and early parenthood development), full of learning and adventure.

Books, though—books littered nearly every aspect of our lives. They were in the car, in the stroller, and in the diaper bag. We read together morning, noon, and night—whenever we needed to connect, felt bored, or thought it would be a nice way to enjoy a picnic. It was no wonder that anyone who visited our home would eventually pick up a book and read with us.

My son was not quite a year old when my cousin Nick moved from Arizona to Montana. He lived with us for about a month while he transitioned into a new job and found a place of his own. Although my cousin was busy, he made time to connect with us after dinner and on weekends. And it was when Nick read a familiar book that my child realized a new quality of the written word.

My cousin opened the book and began to read aloud. My son turned to me with a look of astonishment to which I replied, "I know! He knows the words too." I am as convinced now as I was then that was what my son was thinking. And I believe that was the moment that he really learned the purpose and the power of letters and books. They weren't mine. They were shared with anyone who could understand them.

That was academic preliteracy. But the way books were in our lives was bigger than that. Relationships were built around books, much the way Emilie Buchwald declared, "Children are made readers in the laps of their parents." My lap was the one he sat in the most. But he also read with his father and his grandparents, visitors to our home, and his friends' parents.

To my delight, my son seemed to agree that books (and reading them together) are awesome. He even started to develop a sense that some books are better than others. For example, he loved the mystery and surprise at the end of Donald Crews' Caldecott Honor Book *Freight Train*, where the train seemingly disappears from the page. "Where did it go?" he seemed to ask with his gesture. It seemed clear to me that he was engaged, thoughtful, and interested in the story.

He absolutely loved pint-sized reference books. He would sit with them and pull his toy trucks to match. It seemed like he was curating a mental catalogue of machines: This is my toy bulldozer and here is a picture of a bulldozer; this is my dump truck and here is a picture of a dump truck. Not only was he learning the proper names of the machines, he was also interested in the specialized work they do. So, I sat with him and read the descriptions of the machines and their parts as well as the explanations of the jobs they do.

I was happy for his interest to direct and fuel our inquiry. What's more, his insatiable appetite for learning was infectious and so I also became curious about construction sites. I stopped calling everything a "truck" and began using their proper names. In this way, we learned and developed a common language to communicate about the massive, powerful machines.

Note: Our learning was not achieved with flashcards or drills. It wasn't stuck in books; knowledge was honed through living. For us, in toddlerhood, it looked like playing.

A typical day included a trip to one of the local playgrounds. I would pack the diaper bag with all the accoutrements of early parenthood (diapers, wipes, water, and snacks). Then, together with my son, I would load the stroller with other necessities—a picnic blanket, books, and toys (a dump truck and a front end loader)—and we would walk several blocks to a playground.

More often than not, we went to a place called Bonner Park because it was close, friends could easily meet us there, and it had a lot of sand as well as a splash pad, swings, and an enormous wooden play structure. Surrounded on all four sides by residential properties, Bonner Park was ideal for chasing the garbage truck as it did its rounds on trash day. And, as if that wasn't enough, it was also frequented by the local ice cream truck. I didn't know it at the time, but the three typical features of our trips to the park would follow us for years to come.

One of the first things my child would do when we arrived was get his bearings by running the maze. His tiny legs moved in a blur as he ran up the ramp of the play structure, turned a corner, crossed the bridge, and zigged and zagged his way to the ramp on the other side. Occasionally, he climbed a rope ladder instead of the ramp or rode down a slide as his exit. But, by and large, he followed the same path.

He also always played in the sand. Sometimes, he would get down on all fours and push his bare hands through the sand. I watched as he would lay in the sand and observe it closely. Other times, he would get his front end loader and scoop the sand. Sometimes, he would drive the load up the ramp to the top of the slide and pour it down. Other times, he would drive it to the sidewalk and dump it out. By the day's end, there would be a pile of sand at the bottom of the slide (which I'd brush off) and a dozen or more small piles of sand placed on the cement that marked the edge of the playground's sand.

And, without a doubt, he'd ride on a swing. If there was a bucket swing, then he would use sign language to ask for help in and, of course, I'd push him. If the only swings were for "big kids," then he would ride on my lap. (I would later learn from his occupational therapist that swinging for 15 minutes can help regulate a child for up to 24 hours.)

Between all the play on the ramps, with the sand, and in the swings, I started noticing him doing what I called "playground physics." Not only had he learned rotational-translational motion from playing with his beloved red race car as an infant, it also seemed evident that he was developing some serious visual-spatial awareness by running the maze and getting very comfortable with properties of sand, including how it moves. So, even in toddlerhood, he appeared to be an aspiring self-made expert on force and motion, simple machines, and fluid dynamics. He was (and remains) a playground physicist.

Our days went on like that. We read a lot of books, went to playgrounds, toddled hiking trails, and played with toys. It wasn't until he was two and a half years old that he started to speak.

Unfortunately, his speech sounded like baby babble. His lack of articulation made him incomprehensible. He "spoke" in full sentences, complete with proper intonation—none of which could be understood. One thing led to another and, with the help of a speech therapist, he began to articulate words more clearly. By this time, he was three years old and the things he said surprised us.

One evening, he sat in the bath as part of our typical bedtime routine. As always, he enjoyed closely watching water. He watched it flow from the spout, he scooped it with a cup and dumped it out, he experimented with differently shaped bottles, and he watched water slowly soak a dry washcloth. Then he asked a question that seared into my mind: "Is water like very small sand?"

His father (a physicist) and I (an electrical engineer) were amazed. It seemed to us that our three-year-old had just suggested a model that approximated water molecules with grains of sand. Of course, we realize that water is a liquid and sand is a solid. But typical three-year-olds cannot form an abstract representation of something microscopic. Indeed, we had yet to discover just how atypical he is. Before our son's bath was through, my husband had offered his best three-year-old-friendly explanation of water molecules.

Don't get me wrong. He wasn't a fountain of outstanding observations of the physical and natural world. Most of what he said was typical toddler stuff. He started sharing his observations. "I see a grader!" And, pointing at a box from IKEA, "Hey! That says IKEA." He helped decide which playground to go to, "Let's go to Sand Park." He also talked about what we saw in the books we would read—pointing out letters, shapes, numbers, and finding Goldbug in Richard Scarry's *Cars and Trucks and Things That Go*. He sat in his car seat and recited from memory the spelling of the title of one of his favorite picture books: "D-E-M-O-L-I-T-I-O-N. DEMOLITION!"

So, our lives continued with the privilege of adventure available to upper-middle-class families. We went to the zoo, the children's museum, and the library. We had playdates with our neighbors. We enjoyed installation art, including the Michigan Legacy Art Park, as well as Chihuly at various botanical gardens. There were trips to the grocery store where my son would push the toddler-sized carts around to "help" me. He did gymnastics and took swim lessons. Life was grand.

And sometimes, seemingly out of nowhere, he would surprise us by making a massive leap forward. Case in point—his first train track. For years, we had visited the train table at Barnes & Noble. He would stand and play with the roundhouse or the train wash station. He would push the toy trains around with specific intent to watch them careen down the hill. And, like many families in our circle, we even had our own large set of wooden tracks at home. The thing about our private set that struck me as odd was that he never built with it. Every time we took the tracks out, I would assemble a system, not him.

He was happy to have me building tracks while he did other things. No matter how I invited him, he never joined me. He wouldn't even put two pieces together. He might vote "yea" or "nay" that I would include the tunnel, the bridge, or the splitter in my work, but he never designed his own—not in part or in whole.

Sometimes, it merely seemed curious to me. Why wouldn't he build a train track? Even a simple line or small circle? Other times, I felt frustrated that we had this box of track that he never played with. That is, until one day he knocked it out of the park. I walked into the play room and discovered that he had made a train track system (a closed system at that) that used every single piece of track. He went from never even touching the toy to building a massive and elaborate system that took up more than half the floor space in the not-small room.

My son's curious preoccupations and asynchronous development eventually earned him some labels. He is twice exceptional: His social skills and restrictive repetitive behavior place him in the bottom 2% of children his age, which is labeled "autistic"; his IQ places him in the top 2%, which is labeled "gifted." Those diagnoses provided our family with important insights for understanding him and helped us develop parenting strategies for scaffolding his strengths and his weaknesses.

So, I started reading about autism and giftedness. Sometimes, I found myself weeping over the pages of a book, feeling the relief that comes with finally understanding something peculiar. Other times, I would raise an eyebrow and wonder at the suggestions made—a visual schedule never worked before, why would it now? But a BackJack floor chair? Perhaps, it could solve our circle time woes. My husband and I started to enact recommended strategies and, as in most of the experiment called "parenting," some worked right away, others worked with persistence, and some didn't work at all.

However, for the most part, our lives continued as they had been—filled with books and adventure (although some of the new adventures were to work with occupational therapists and speech therapists).

It was after one such new adventure that I felt perplexed. The speech therapist (a woman I trust and respect) came to me and described something that concerned her. They had gone on a letter hunt for the letter M and my son had pointed out not only the M's but the W's as well. At the time, I didn't understand why that would be cause for concern. In fact, I thought it was quite clever that he had been able to spot the M's in disguise. Now I understand that it was indicative of the challenges he'd face decoding letters.

The diagnoses didn't change who my child was; they simply gave us a clue that he was experiencing the world markedly differently from 99.5% of children his age. Case in point—those profound physics epiphanies. They continued to happen year after year. When he was four years old, he asked, "Is electricity like very small water?" And, at age five, "If the earth is spinning, then why don't we fly off?"

These spontaneous and insightful questions arose as if from nowhere— offered up in the hushed moments before bedtime or while digging quietly in the sandbox. They were never related to the most recent topic of conversation, which seemed to make them all the more brilliant.

By the time he was ready to start public school, he appeared to be a poster child for early intervention. He could speak intelligibly; he looked at people when he spoke and when they spoke to him; his nutrition was homemade and wholesome; he was remarkably self-aware; when his sensory needs were met and his preoccupations given time to be explored, he was a willing and able student. He *loved* being around other people. (And I looked forward to being that much closer to getting a job again.) School could be the newest adventure—or not.

I was struck by the narrow focus of our first IEP meeting. The team ignored two-thirds of my son's medical developmental assessment (phonological disorder, gifted) and concentrated on autism. I now know that they, in fact, completely disregarded the medical diagnoses and skipped the 504, focusing only on their own educational assessment to create an IEP. I was told, "We are only discussing his ability to participate in school life," the subtext to which was, "We aren't interested in his ability to function outside of school." They also told me, "If you don't attend your neighborhood school, then we cannot guarantee services." My lively and charismatic child was reduced to a label and treated like a misunderstood deviant.

At the same time, we gained access to more interventions, including therapeutic karate, yoga, and handwriting. This meant more time in the car and so we added audio stories to our reading—some do it yourself, some professionally produced books, and even a few operas.

Outside of school, my son was thriving. He had great relationships with his karate classmates, his coaches, and his tutors. He formed relationships with local musicians. When he started public school, the rich, spontaneous, and whole child way of life was reduced to checklists. He knew most of the letters and their sounds, and he could count. That was the long and short of his existence.

He made it through kindergarten (three hours per day, five days per week) fairly unscathed but only passing his standardized tests by the skin of his teeth. And, yet, he still enjoyed sitting with a book.

First grade was an entirely different story. I was told that there was no programming for gifted students until third grade. I also received some raised eyebrows when I confessed that, no, my son can't read. And that common indicator of giftedness (early reading) slapped me in the face: If he can't read, then he's certainly not gifted.

It took six months of first grade to obliterate his spirit. He started having tantrums that lasted most of his waking hours at home. He cried. He claimed that he didn't deserve love. Then, he began eloping from school. There was no longer time for books or adventures; our time was spent trying to manage his meltdowns and work with the school to remedy the cause of his paralyzing struggles.

I tried to be patiently impatient with the school. I offered solutions, I volunteered to build a program, I was open and honest, and I requested a paraprofessional. Emails were sent, phone calls were made, and special meetings were held while administrators and educators hurriedly pantomimed their way through the motions to brainstorm how to meet my son's needs without straining their system, taking so long afterward to implement agreed-upon interventions that he would develop a whole new set of challenges. Meanwhile, my son, a mere seven years old, descended into depression.

Eventually, we were advised by a trusted professional who was familiar with autism, twice exceptionality, and the school district to make a choice: either sue the school for child abuse or disenroll him and find a different plan for educating him. We chose the latter. Slowly, but steadily, his health improved and he began to move confidently through the world again.

Now we are back to living a life full of adventure and books. And you know what? He recently turned eight years old and he can read. His current favorite books to read aloud are by Anna Kang. They are simple picture books that tell engaging stories about lovable characters. They are probably not considered "age appropriate," but they are developmentally appropriate for him. He is ready to face the letters and words on the page with confidence—and so he does.

He also sits quietly with reference books about Minecraft or other subjects of interest. When he's reading those, I'm sometimes asked to read important passages that he can't quite figure out on his own.

Of course, audiobooks are still a *huge* presence in our lives. These days, he is binging on a newly discovered series called *Wings of Fire* by Tui T. Sutherland—300-page books that, when read aloud, run approximately eight hours.

He loves good stories—long and short. Cognitively, he can understand and enjoy lengthy, complicated books. But, when using his eyes to read, he is easily fatigued so short and sweet is better. Both ways of enjoying books are valid. Both ways are important. Both ways are part of our daily life. We no longer both fit on the antique rocking chair, but that other aspect of reading is preserved in our homeschool: Books bring us together.

The other day, he was having a hard time. There was no obvious explanation for his explosiveness. My husband and I brainstormed about half a dozen equally plausible ideas, including growth spurt, developmental burst, and jealousy that his younger sister was rapidly learning to read and write. Whatever the cause, I struggled to parent with patience and flexibility for an entire seven hours before my son and I collapsed together on the couch at 1 p.m.

He scowled at me. I suggested, "Want to read a book together? Sometimes that helps." "OK," he reluctantly replied. I held *I Am (Not) Scared* between us. He began to read aloud without me asking. And, as if by magic, he began to smile. With each turn of a page, his smile got bigger. By the end, he said, "Ah.

That worked! I feel better." His shoulders had relaxed and he seemed lighter, ready to get off the couch and go play, which is exactly what he did. So, the relationship built around books remains intact.

I never really worried that my child wouldn't learn to read. I believe that all children will learn to read when they are ready. It will happen organically and be done with enthusiasm. All they need is time, space, and an environment filled with interesting (to them) books and book lovers.

Only the school pathologized my child's way of learning to read because it was out of sync with what they expected/needed in terms of speed, timing, and rhythm. However, for children who are wildly asynchronous, like he is, reading readiness is tricky business; it should be approached with flexibility, imagination, and boatloads of patience.

And, now, it is with great joy that I celebrate the light at the end of this tunnel (one of many on the road of parenting)! My son is gifted, he is autistic, and he can finally read.

Imagine a World Where Gifted Kids Don't Have to Wait

PAULA PROBER

It all started in first grade when you eagerly finished the entire workbook in one night. You thought your teacher would be pleased. They were not pleased. You were told to sit and color the pictures and *wait* until the other first graders caught up with you.

Then there was the time they were teaching addition and you had been doing complicated calculations in your head since you were four. You were told to *wait*. You were too young to learn fractions.

When you were 11, you were dying to read *The Autobiography of Malcolm X*, but you were told to *wait*. That was the book everyone was required to read in high school.

When you scored in the 99th percentile in reading and math and could easily work two years above grade level, it was decided that you shouldn't skip a grade. You needed to *wait* until you were more emotionally and socially mature, even though you were capable of contributing confidently to discussions with your parents' friends.

You wanted to know about death and God. You were told to *wait* until you were a grown-up because you wouldn't understand.

You're still waiting.

Your colleagues at work take hours to conclude what you knew last week.

Your boss wants you to calm down and slow down and not share your ideas just yet. Maybe next week.

You've completed all of your assigned work for the day and it's only 1 p.m.

Your supervisor says they'll get back to you with the answers to your questions. They never do.

You've learned everything you can about your job and now the tasks are frustrating and boring.

You wonder when you can share the fascinating article you read in *The New Yorker* while friends talk about recipes and reality TV.

You have so much to say about so many things but you have to find the right time to speak so that you don't overwhelm your partner, friends, relatives, children, and pets with your enthusiasm, sensitivities, and ideas. (Well, OK, maybe your pets aren't overwhelmed.)

Waiting. Waiting. Waiting.

In his book *The Boy Who Played with Fusion*, Tom Clynes wrote:

> *Waiting* was the most common response when Tracy Cross of the College of William and Mary asked thirteen thousand kids in seven states to describe in one word their experience as gifted children.[7]

13,000 kids. Waiting.

Imagine a world where gifted kids don't have to *wait*. A world where you can be yourself. Imagine the possibilities. I want to live in that world.

College Planning and Your Gifted Child: Start Early, Plan Wisely

GAIL POST, PhD

Raising a gifted child is full of surprises. Emotional intensity, asynchronous development, and navigating school policy are just a few of the challenges parents face. And, just when you think you have it figured out and life gets a little more predictable, college looms.

But why would this be difficult? After all, getting into college should be a piece of cake for your child. *Right?*

The Nagging Reality of College Admissions

Many parents of gifted children are blindsided by the competitive nature of college admissions. While your child may shine in high school, there are more valedictorians, National Merit Finalists, varsity athletes, and science fair winners, for example, than openings at selective colleges. And, despite media criticism of selective, elite colleges, these schools often provide the best fit for gifted students—where their intellectual abilities are appreciated and classrooms are finally filled with like-minded peers.

In my work as a psychologist, I have spoken with frustrated, bewildered, and sometimes heartbroken teens and families who felt betrayed and misled by their high school and deceived by the general hype about colleges. Many parents assume that their highly ranked child will automatically gain admission to the school of their choice and are stunned when the subsequent rejection letter is received—delivered to thousands of other equally accomplished applicants as well. They regret trusting their child's judgment or relying on the school guidance counselors to figure it out and wish they had started planning much earlier.

How Students' College Dreams Get Sidelined

Many families learn much too late that the school offers little guidance, especially for gifted children. Overworked guidance counselors may have accrued college information relevant for the majority of students but offer little direction for gifted students. And some parents—who might have micromanaged every birthday party and routinely monitored their teen's activities—suddenly abandon all responsibility when it comes to college planning.

Yet, placing full responsibility for such a critical decision on your child (at an age when many teens understandably lack a certain level of maturity) can be a recipe for disaster. How many teens have chosen a college because of its reputation as a party school, or because their friends like it, or because they think the school's prestige is essential for their self-esteem? How many high-achieving children dream of attending Harvard or Stanford or MIT, even when the odds are against them? How many 17-year-olds truly understand the financial issues involved, including what you can really afford, the burden of loans, and whether a particular college is even worth the cost? *How many teens can assess these variables without your input?*

I also wish I had known what I know now—*before* my children started high school. Fortunately, once my oldest child was in high school, I realized the importance of educating myself about the process. The school offered no roadmap and little guidance. Online tips about college planning did not necessarily apply to gifted children's needs. While my children ultimately made their own decisions, it fell upon us as parents to "suggest" what classes, tests, and activities seemed advantageous and which colleges might provide the best fit for their academic, social, and financial needs.

How Can You Help Your Child Plan for College—and Find Colleges That Offer the Right Fit?

Gifted teens thrive in a college environment that pushes them to stretch themselves, instills a work ethic, and encourages inquiry and creative expression. Most welcome the opportunity to finally excel without fear of social repercussions. Finding a college with the right fit that fosters this growth and development is essential for all teens, but it is *especially* critical for gifted students. What follows are a few guidelines.

Educate Yourself about the Planning Process—and Start Early

Put aside any expectations of fully relying on the school for guidance, or that you can wait until your child's junior year to start planning, or that your child can make a clearheaded decision without your input. It will fall upon you to investigate admissions requirements at selected colleges and what these institutions can offer your child. You also need to understand the relative importance of the PSAT, dual enrollment, AP classes, extracurricular activities, SAT or ACT preparation, and how colleges weigh these factors in admissions decisions. Take note of the benefits or drawbacks of early action and early decision applications and whether supplementary material (such as a publication or an audition tape) could make a difference.

Encourage your child to take the most challenging classes available in high school and offer some input into identifying extracurricular, volunteer, and academic choices that may boost the odds of admission. Colleges are alert to "filler" activities, though, which some students use to pad their applications, such as joining a variety of clubs that have little connection to their interests. On the other hand, dual enrollment at a local college, internships, and meaningful volunteer work are examples of activities that offer enrichment and appeal to college admissions officers as well.

Learn the Hidden Meaning behind the Words of Admissions Departments

Most colleges market themselves based on their reputation and what they believe will spark interest among prospective applicants. Some try to boost their status by cultivating a low acceptance rate, which can be inflated through a greater proportion of applications to acceptances. In other words, the flood of emails and postcards your child may receive encouraging applications does not necessarily translate into a sure bet for admissions. Colleges also maintain a profile of the type of student they would like to enroll. While they may list strict admissions criteria, there is some subjectivity, which makes odds of admission hard to predict. Admissions departments from highly selective colleges often speak of "holistic" admissions and identifying applicants who will add to a well-rounded class. When GPA or SAT score ranges are listed, be advised that unless your child fits what some describe as "hooked" (such as recruited athlete or legacy status), grades and scores should correspond with numbers in the top percentile for consideration.

If your child plans to apply to a highly selective college, great grades and SAT scores are not enough. Applicants need to distinguish themselves from the rest of the pack. An exceptional accomplishment (such as publication in a scientific journal) or a combination of achievements (National Merit Finalist, captain of the tennis team, lead role in the musical, completion of several college classes, and volunteering in a university chemistry lab) will help your child get noticed. The more you know about what colleges realistically expect and how that corresponds with your child's specific accomplishments, the more easily you can help your child determine a realistic list of prospective colleges.

Evaluate Online, Word-of-Mouth, and College Website Information within the Context of Giftedness

Information about college planning, admissions, and the college itself is geared toward all students and may not be relevant to your gifted child's unique needs. Selling points that many colleges promote—sports teams, beautiful dorms, a new performing arts building, an appealing study abroad program— are attractive but can distract from what is critical when determining if the college can meet your child's academic and social/emotional needs.

Parents and teens benefit from visiting prospective colleges when possible. Separate what you can overlook (the tour guide's demeanor) from what is essential information (how your child can show "demonstrated interest"). It is ideal if your child can ask permission to sit in on a few classes and observe extracurricular activities of interest. For example, if club sports, marching band, or dance is critical to your child's well-being, observing these activities can offer essential information about whether the college is a good fit. Find out as many details about academic requirements as possible and ask your child to envision day-to-day life there. Red flags might include a long list of general education requirements; a weak honors program; few opportunities for collaborative research with faculty; large, "stadium-seating" classes; or classes mostly taught by teaching assistants. Some colleges also make it difficult for students with multiple interests to double major in certain fields. For example, music ensemble or theater practice may conflict with the schedule for science labs, making it almost impossible to double major in these areas.

Understand Your Child's Needs and the Importance of "Fit"

Most of us understand the importance of fit even though it might seem like one of those vague, murky concepts that defies definition. Helping your gifted teen sort out and rank what is essential, what is ideal, and what expectations can be sacrificed will optimize the chance of finding the right fit. While you might set limits on costs or geographic distance from home, allow your child the freedom to identify what is most important. For example, many teens hold strong opinions regarding an urban or rural location, the relative importance of school spirit and sports, the presence or absence of Greek life, the local weather, and the size of the school. And these preferences should be honored. On the other hand, your child may not be cognizant of factors extending beyond freshman year, such as housing availability and affordability over the course of all four years or the quality of the college's job placement services available prior to graduation. It will fall upon you to raise these practical considerations.

Take Your Financial Status into Account

Unfortunately, some students are accepted into their dream school and then are devastated to find that their parents cannot afford the tuition. Wishful thinking may lead families to assume that their child will receive a merit scholarship sufficient to cover most of their costs or that website financial aid estimators are wrong. It is critical to realistically assess what is affordable and inform your child before setting sights on any specific school. While elite colleges typically provide the most generous need-based financial aid, this will not help some middle- and upper-middle-class families. And take note of the difference between colleges that support need-blind policies (where admissions officers are not influenced by a student's financial status) and those with need-aware policies (where a student's demonstrated financial need can be considered in the decision-making process).

If you cannot afford (or oppose the idea of paying) the high cost of tuition at a selective college that does not offer financial support, consider an honors college at your state university or a college that will welcome your child with significant merit-based aid. And keep in mind that some colleges offer a "free ride" of full tuition and room and board to certain applicants, particularly those who are National Merit Finalists (which is another reason to encourage your child to perform well on the PSAT in 11th grade).

Be the Voice of Reality

It falls on you to be the adult in the room. You know your child's abilities and potential and hope that colleges will recognize these qualities as well. But colleges have specific criteria and quotas, and admissions officers focus on what is visible on the application, not necessarily potential. You might hope that dream school will overlook the C in biology or a less-than-stellar SAT math score. But, with thousands of equally qualified students applying to the school, your child may be shut out.

Too many students apply to "reach" schools, refuse to consider colleges that are more likely to be "matches," and end up attending the one "safety" school they applied to in haste. Parents are sometimes reluctant to squash their child's dreams by redirecting them to a college that is a better fit. There are many wonderful colleges to consider. And you can encourage your child to apply to those that are likely to offer admission *and* provide a meaningful and challenging education, even if they are not dream schools.

Help Your Child Make This Happen

Both of my children were fortunate to emerge relatively unscathed from the college application process. They encountered a few bumps along the way but also some surprises and amazing opportunities, and they enrolled in colleges that were well suited to their different needs. My kids put in the effort to apply, but I doubt they would have had as many options without some direction from us as parents.

Unless your child's high school has an exceptionally astute guidance department, unhurried and unburdened by an enormous caseload of students and with an understanding of gifted students' needs, I urge you to become informed and involved. Start the conversation early. Learn as much as possible from information online, books, college websites, parent forums, advice from other parents of gifted teens and college students, and conversations with trusted professionals involved in your child's education and development. Remaining informed, offering your own wise counsel, and staying involved is not hovering—as long as you respect and stay attuned to your child's (realistic) wishes. Your child will appreciate your efforts when finally enrolled at a college that offers the best possible academic, social, and financial fit.

PART FOUR
2eeek!

For others, it's different aspects of development that are out of whack: They can read but not write, or recite the periodic table but not toilet train, or calculate orbital trajectories in their heads but still need to co-sleep. The point is the lows that come with the highs and the vertiginous zipping between the two.

—*Rebecca Farley*

Distinguishing Sensory Issues from Other Disorders in Children

TERESA CURRIVAN

Sensory processing issues can be misunderstood and misdiagnosed as a number of things, most commonly attention-deficit/hyperactivity disorder (ADHD), oppositional defiant disorder (ODD), and anxiety disorders. In my opinion, it is necessary to rule out any sensory issues or address them as thoroughly as possible before considering other diagnoses.

Does your child seem agitated and are they agitating to be around? Or, conversely, do they avoid being with others and seem to shut down when they would really like to connect? Usually, our kids want to do things right—to listen, sit still, control their impulses, be a member of the group—but sometimes they are unable to. This can be frustrating for children, especially when they are blamed for such behavior.

In my practice, I see many kids like this. They appear to have signs of ADHD when, in reality, they may be experiencing something entirely different. Some of the behaviors may be part of these children's hardwiring, but the sudden outbursts, the inability to control impulses, or the intolerance of any noise in the room could also indicate sensory processing issues. I highly recommend getting children checked for sensory issues before anything else. (If they do have ADHD, for example, it is best to clear out sensory issues to accurately get help for the ADHD. If they have anxiety, you may see that diminished by thoroughly addressing the sensory issues.)

Sensory processing issues are often misunderstood. They have more to do with how the brain processes the senses rather than the senses themselves. Children with sensory processing issues can be either sensory seekers or sensory avoiders. For example, a child may make loud sounds in order to hear the reverberation in their head that they are craving because their brain has not registered certain pitches of sound. Alternatively, a child might find the seams in their socks intolerable because their brain is receiving too much stimulation. Both of these could be going on within the same child.

To further complicate things, standard visual and hearing exams will not necessarily indicate problems. In fact, visual and auditory issues are often missed. Most exams for vision and hearing at schools and in doctors' offices do not test for deeper visual and auditory issues.

If sensory issues are found, addressing these issues as thoroughly as possible with appropriate therapies is vital. Vision therapy is quite effective when followed through with and done regularly. I have seen a child who was very resistant to vision therapy (because it made them nauseous) suddenly become more open to it and advance significantly after their vestibular issues were addressed. The correct sensory therapies will reconnect wiring in the brain that is out of balance, solving the problem at its core. Only once that is done can you or a professional see more clearly if there are other issues. (A child cannot receive tutoring for dyslexia while there are unresolved vision issues; that is like teaching a child to run without first mending their broken leg.)

An example is Jane. She seems jumpy, has difficulty reading, and tends to lack an appropriate "space bubble" around her (she gets a little too close to friends and knocks things over accidentally). She consistently tested as having 20/20 vision. But, through testing with a certified developmental optometrist, it was discovered that she has esotropia (one eye turned in at times) and tracking issues (difficulty finding words on a page when looking from left to right). Once her issues were identified and she received vision therapy, she was able to control herself. Her mother reported that she was "so much more grounded." While she may still have ADHD, she appears much less agitated and has her self-esteem back because she is no longer agitating to others.

Another child, Dennis, was very loud at inappropriate times; seemed agitated internally, especially in noisy environments; and was annoying to others around him. Sometimes, he requested to be in a room by himself; other times, he joined the group but became loud and aggressive. Similarly, his mom reported that he would begin yelling when a blender or vacuum was turned on. The paradox is that he may have been yelling to match the noise he perceived in order to tolerate it: He yelled as a coping mechanism in response to the overwhelm the loud noise made him feel. While he was thought to have a problem with his ears, he tested as having good hearing. After proper testing, it turned out Dennis had central auditory processing disorder, which made him unable to filter noises properly. He heard distant noises as if they were close; but, unless he was looking at her lips, he did not hear his mother's voice when she was standing directly in front of him. His brain needed to be retrained to hear appropriately. After completing auditory therapy, he became more grounded, no longer shouting at odd times. Now, when his mother talks to him and he "doesn't hear," he jokes, "Oh, now I hear you. I was just ignoring you." At least it has become his choice and he has kept his sense of humor.

An important point to make here is that these therapies can be intense for some kids and can temporarily exacerbate behaviors. At one point, Dennis stopped auditory therapy because he was very resistant to it. At about the same time, his challenging behavior escalated. I urged his parents to continue the therapy and helped Dennis find exercises that could integrate his auditory system with his other systems. His challenging behaviors became more manageable and he was able to continue.

As a parent of a twice-exceptional child, I know that all of the therapies and diagnoses can be overwhelming. While we want the best for our children, many of our brains and budgets are overstretched. As a professional trained to diagnose children in mental health settings, I know that sensory issues can look like any number of other pathologies. I urge parents to look into sensory issues first and foremost before accepting a diagnosis of ADHD, ODD, or anxiety. Considering and addressing sensory concerns, rather than being an additional step, can actually solve many behavioral issues more efficiently and properly than more common treatments. This may lead to a more grounded, peaceful child who can manage their world. It may even make your world more manageable.

Why Sensory Processing Disorder Makes Everything Hard and a Phrase That Makes Things Easier

JULIE SCHNEIDER

I have a memory of my son when he was two years old that has stuck with me over time. He was doing one of his favorite things—pushing a dump truck at top speed back and forth in our cul-de-sac. He had figured out a way to balance perfectly with his hands resting on the bed in a manner that didn't let the bed flip up while he ran behind (a feat other children didn't realize until they tried to race their dump trucks too).

What he hadn't figured out was how to keep an eye out for the terrain in front of him. The front wheels caught on a crack in the pavement and my son went silently end over end. He stood up, grabbed his truck, and started pushing again.

"Whoa!" said a neighbor child. "He's tough."

I didn't realize how tough he was until he came racing by me and I saw blood dripping down his legs and arms. When he had landed, the asphalt had taken a good deal of skin off his knees and elbows, yet he didn't seem to notice. So, I corralled him to clean his wounds quickly but carefully before unleashing him back into the street to play.

That's what it's been like for me to parent a young child with sensory processing disorder (SPD). I am constantly trying to figure out what his needs are because it doesn't seem like he knows them himself. He is undersensitive, or a "seeker," constantly seeking more information by touching things, mouthing them, moving his body, overstuffing his mouth, etc. He has trouble anticipating sneezing, bowel movements, or vomit. He doesn't feel pain until a bone is broken, nor does he feel hunger until he is hangry.

At home, it's easy to stick to our routines. For years, I have anticipated food needs and prepared snacks that are ready to eat whether we are approaching snack time at home or at a playground. However, when we travel, routines with food are not as easy to maintain. That, combined with frazzling travel logistics, means I am often faced with a hangry child.

It was when my son was six years old and we were on a family vacation that we were able to turn a corner with regard to self-regulation and food. My son came to me screaming that he was hungry. He was upset and stressed. Old enough to understand that I am separate from him, he was finally able to comprehend that I did not know that his body needed food.

"I didn't know you were hungry," I said.

"Well, you should have known," he replied.

"You're used to me anticipating your hunger and having things ready."

"Yeah."

"But I didn't this time. In the future, will you please come to me and say, 'Mama, I'm hungry. Let's make a healthy snack together.'"

"OK!" he smiled. Then together we fetched a plate from my sister's cabinet and prepared a snack.

From that day forward, I felt like I had found a new nugget of gold to keep close at hand as a parent: "Let's do it together."

It seems so simple to say, but it isn't.

I've found this phrase particularly useful when something is challenging one of my children, which usually coincides with when I'm running out of patience: I have asked 10 times for someone to put on their shoes, or pick up some toys, or clear the table, or get dressed, or do their copywork, or fill the water bottles, or...

When one of my children is dragging their heels, the *best* thing I can do is to help. I take a deep breath, count to 10, tie on my cape, and say, "Let's do it together."

As soon as I offer help, the task is monumentally easier and everyone wins. The job gets done, and I show my children that I am there to offer help when they need it, especially when they don't even know to ask.

Asking for help falls under executive function. A child has to have working memory to recognize that they are struggling with something; they have to have enough mental flexibility to imagine that someone else might be able to help; and they have to have enough self-control to pause what they are doing, find someone who might help, and ask for assistance.

That seems like a tall order for a young child, made even taller by SPD. If their brains are not processing physical stimuli, then how can they properly assess the situation and their needs, let alone employ working memory, mental flexibility, and self-control? And, as we all know, if someone's needs are not being met, then everything else falls apart.

The tough thing for a child with SPD is that they might not know that their needs are not met. That means that parenting these children comes with unique responsibilities. A child with SPD does not have normal signals from their body, so teaching self-care (such as cleaning a cut, eating when hungry, or resting) requires special attention and deliberate instruction.

"Let's do it together" is a simple phrase that helps everyone slow down and work together to accomplish difficult tasks. By collaborating on the challenging stuff, I am able to point out what is hard and bring my son's attention to it, thus teaching him how to identify when he is injured, hungry, tired, or must otherwise take care of his physical needs.

Working together makes tough situations less so—for everyone. And, slowly but surely, we (yes, we) create and maintain a supportive, reliable relationship with one another.

ADHD and Giftedness: It's Complicated

KATHLEEN HUMBLE

I've been trying for a long time to figure out a quick and easy way of explaining the complex interaction of attention-deficit/hyperactivity disorder (ADHD) and giftedness.

It's actually caused a lot of sleepless nights, courtesy of my own ADHD, hyperfocus, and inability to actually finish anything. Hopefully, what I offer here will help clarify the connection.

How Many Gifted Kids Have ADHD?

To begin, it's important to note that we don't know how many gifted kids have ADHD. At present, it looks like that number is lower than or the same as the total number of neurotypical children with the same condition.

But there's a problem. In a manner similar to the guidelines for autism, the diagnostic criteria for ADHD were determined using boys of average IQ. That's important because girls with ADHD behave in ways that differ from those exhibited by boys with ADHD. Girls exhibit less hyperactivity; they talk more and are more likely to be inattentive rather than hyperactive. And gifted boys with ADHD can possess these same traits. This alone flags a problem with the rate of ADHD diagnoses in gifted kids: They don't necessarily look like stereotypical boys with ADHD. For many gifted kids with ADHD, their hyperactivity is in their brain—not their body. So, they may never get referred for testing.

This is even greater in the case of gifted girls with ADHD. I was in my late 30s before I was identified—and that only happened after both of my kids were diagnosed. I sat through dozens of sessions with specialists explaining how my kids' behaviors were ADHD related. At first, I thought, "Well, isn't that normal?" Then I realized, yes, it was normal for me because I have ADHD too. After a lot of dithering (hello ADHD!), when I finally got to a specialist for my own diagnosis, I found out I wasn't just ADHD—I was *stereotypical ADHD*.

I never climbed the walls as a kid. Well, not after I fell and sprained my knee badly enough for crutches. I was a quiet kid. It took five-plus seconds to get my attention. It's my auditory buffer. It lags.

I passed my tests. And I handed in assignments. Granted, I usually did them on the day they were due. In fact, on one memorable occasion, I handed in an assignment laced with the aroma of the rotting banana I had forgotten was in my bag. I had to scrape it off the paper. But I got an A+ on that one.

Gifted ADHD kids won't necessarily be failing. If they are highly gifted, they might even look mostly functional—until they don't.

Working Memory Differences

It gets more complicated, because, even if we know what we're looking for, the red flags aren't the same.

Gifted boys with ADHD don't have low working memory scores. (This most probably also pertains to girls, but getting together enough gifted girls with ADHD for a study is *hard*.) I'll repeat that: Gifted kids with ADHD have average working memory scores. This is important, because a deficit of working memory (how much information you can hold in your brain at one time) is a hallmark of ADHD. If a child's working memory is impaired, but not well below average, the chances of ADHD being discovered with a quick screening test are low.

But, hey, average is OK, right? Not really. Average indicates that these kids are using their unusual brains to compensate for greater deficits. When properly tested, gifted kids with ADHD will exhibit extremely poor working memory, processing speed, and auditory verbal memory relative to their other abilities. It's extreme asynchrony on steroids. Kids like this want to do and understand complicated things, but they can't hold onto the necessary information, they can't follow conversation, and it takes them way longer to figure out what someone is saying.

I know what that's like. I have spent my entire life reconstructing conversations that I haven't actually heard. My brain skips. I have to guess what people are talking about. And, more often than not, I figure out what an "appropriate" response sounds like and fake it. Sometimes, I can logic my way back to what was said. Sometimes, I can't. It sucks.

Even if gifted kids with ADHD score well, we have to remember that the score is *not* the diagnosis. It is a way to find kids who have ADHD. The mental health implications are the same for all kids with ADHD: Living with a brain that most people consider "wrong" or "lazy" is not fun. After a while, these children start to internalize the constant criticism, "If you're so smart, why can't you do this?"

When looked at from a neurotypical point of view, a lot of the things ADHD individuals can't do look easy. Surely *anyone* can do them, right? I wish.

ADHD and Giftedness Destructively Interact

It can be easy to think of giftedness and ADHD "canceling" out each other. And, for some things, such as verbal working memory, that can happen; the gifted brain compensates and brings the deficits up to average. But, for other symptoms, that's not the case. For gifted kids with ADHD, the social difficulties are actually worse than they are for those kids of average IQ who also have ADHD. Instead of acting as a buffer, the emotional and social differences for gifted kids with ADHD destructively interact.

This actually makes a lot of sense. ADHD comes with executive functioning deficits. Executive functioning is one of the ways the brain helps us control our impulses and emotions.

Gifted kids' brains have a greater emotional reaction to situations; it's visible in their brains under functional magnetic resonance imaging, which measures brain activity by detecting changes associated with blood flow. It's also why gifted kids often remember things better. Emotions trigger memory formation. But that also means that they react to situations more intensely. Gifted kids with ADHD have less brain "brakes" than neurotypical kids—and a faster car. So, the possibility of crashes increases greatly.

Kids with ADHD often don't "get" kids that don't have ADHD, and social constructs can be much harder to navigate. Add an extra layer of neurodifference—giftedness—and the social disconnect grows exponentially. Inject a dose of "Well, I know how that works!" gifted brain-ness and a lack of impulse control ADHD-ness, and it's a perfect storm.

Complicated but Worth Exploring

There are many similarities between giftedness and ADHD, and some good research has been conducted.[1,2] It's not simply an either/or situation. For both the impacted kids and their parents, a proper full diagnosis can make a world of difference. It certainly did for my children and me.

Is My Gifted Child Autistic?

KATHLEEN HUMBLE

I've done lots of reading, I've looked at the standard definitions, I've listened to the niggles and problems that different people—my general practitioner, a friend, my child's teacher, etc.—have mentioned. I know my child's quirky, but is my gifted child autistic?

It's a question almost every parent of gifted kids I've ever talked to has asked at one time or another (particularly the parents of highly to profoundly gifted children). And though it seems there should be an easy answer to this question—a quick test, a definitive way of responding yes or no—the answer is actually much more complicated.

As one who has been descending into this rabbit hole for a long while now, I invite you to join me on a trip into the world of giftedness and autism.

To start, despite organized checklists, the answer isn't clear-cut.[3] There are no easy-to-complete lists, and there are many overlapping characteristics that depend for their interpretation on the eye of the beholder (for example, the difference between hyperlexia and precocious reading).[4]

My own experience with my son is a good illustration: He was an extremely precocious reader, sightreading words by his second birthday but lagging in his comprehension of what he read depending on the topic. Factual material, even complicated scientific ideas, was not just comprehended but chewed, swallowed, and reinterpreted. He really understood what he was reading. (And still does. I have on more than one occasion found him immersed in reading some of his father's or my old college textbooks.)

But he struggled with fiction; stories that relied on interpreting emotional undertones went completely over his head. His challenges couldn't quite be attributed to hyperlexia, but they did illustrate his problems understanding social interactions. Determining whether his emotional comprehension of material was age appropriate, hyperlexic, or a broader social comprehension problem was far more difficult.

It can be hard to determine where giftedness "stops" and autism "starts." Or even if that is a sensible way to think about the problem. (This piece specifically focuses on gifted children. Just as gifted children are a small minority of the general population, gifted autistic kids are a minority of the gifted population.[5])

Where To Start

We must first acknowledge that it takes some serious professionally qualified nous to answer this question.

Current research suggests that to even have a chance of obtaining an accurate answer, not just a psychologist but, at a minimum, a clinical or educational and developmental psychologist is needed. These extra qualifications can take up to 10 years of additional study to acquire. It's also a good idea to ensure that the chosen professional has experience with testing both gifted and autistic children.[6]

But merely performing an IQ test isn't enough. When researchers at the Belin–Blank Center at the University of Iowa tested 81 gifted children, with half previously diagnosed as also being autistic, they found that there was little to no difference in the IQ results for both groups.[7]

When IQ tests are the only prescreening tool used, there's a good chance many gifted autistic children will be missed. In fact, according to this research, the only set of tests currently available able to reliably screen for most (but not all) gifted autistic children is the full ADOS (Autism Diagnostic Observation Schedule) and, in particular, the BASC-3 (Behavior Assessment System for Children) and the Vineland-II.[8,9,10,11,12] Both of these are questionnaires for parents and teachers on behavioral characteristics and are the tools best able to accurately distinguish between the gifted and autistic groups.

Even still, though the researchers were able to determine a statistical difference between the two groups, there were problems. Some of the gifted autistic children ended up in the gifted range. And some of the gifted but not autistic kids ended up in the gifted autistic range. The researchers were able to distinguish between the groups en masse, but that didn't mean their findings were always accurate.

Why Is It Hard?

One of the reasons it's so hard to answer this question is that the characteristics of gifted children and autistic children really are similar—at least when looked at from the outside using behavioral studies. If you're trying to determine if your gifted child is also autistic, finding the bits of their behavior or thinking that are measurably different from just giftedness is like finding a needle in a haystack, in the dark, with your hands tied behind your back.

The problems with separating the two are compounded by the fact that research into giftedness and research into autism have been conducted almost completely separately for an awfully long time. No one was checking for overlap. No one was even looking much at all.

It wasn't until the new millennium that researchers had their "call to arms" moment and really started taking a good look at whether it was easy or hard to distinguish gifted kids from gifted autistic kids.[13] Until that point (and, indeed, still in much clinical practice), the diagnosis a child received depended on the specialty of the assessing professional—professionals with experience with autistic children were more likely to assess a gifted child as autistic, and professionals with experience with gifted children were more likely to assess a child as gifted but not autistic.[14]

It wasn't until recently that research into gifted autistic children moved much beyond individual case studies.[15] And the first truly comprehensive study with a large enough sample for the creation of diagnostic criteria was only performed as recently as 2014.[16]

What Does the Research Say?

The latest research, done at the University of Groningen in 2014, actually seems to suggest that we're asking the wrong question when we try to find an exact "cutoff" point between autistic and nonautistic gifted children.[17]

Instead, these researchers recommend a whole-child approach that assesses the strengths and weaknesses of each child and develops strategies to help them in their specific areas of need. In this model, there is no cutoff point, because the relationship between giftedness and autism isn't linear but, much like both giftedness and autism, is a spectrum of characteristics that aren't easy to separate. It's called the "S&W Heuristic."[18]

Gifted Autistic Girls

Of course, even this cutting-edge research has gaps and includes questions that have yet to be answered. One of the more pressing is about gifted autistic girls. Among the problems that have been identified in the current research into autism (and there are many) is the lack of screening procedures and characteristic behavioral tests for autistic girls who have average to above average IQs.[19] This has led to an underdiagnosis of autistic girls, who may have a greater ability to mask their autism, and to the current 3:1 ratio of autistic boys compared to autistic girls.[20]

This has been and will probably continue to be an ongoing diagnostic problem for the foreseeable future. Unfortunately, much of the research on gifted autistic children relies on these norms. Even the developers of the S&W Heuristic, which as of 2014 was the best method for diagnosing gifted autistic individuals, used the 3:1 ratio for boys and girls in their development of testing procedures.[21]

In almost all the current research on gifted autistic kids, the number of gifted autistic girls represented in the research sample is less than 10, often being as low as 5. And this, sadly, is potentially too small for the kind of rigorous statistical analysis that would be needed for the use of this research in clinical practice.

Prodigy and Autism

One last complicating wrinkle in the research fabric of giftedness and autism is in the work done by researchers at Ohio University on the link between prodigy and autism.[22] They have conducted a number of studies, including case studies, behavioral studies, and genetic testing, for a significant number of prodigies and their extended families. (Considering how rare prodigy is, this is quite an achievement in and of itself.)

According to these researchers, characteristics that are considered as core identifying features of autism—extreme focus and extraordinary attention to detail in very specific (and possibly obscure) fields—are actually more evident and intense in prodigies. There also appear to be a greater number of autistic individuals in the extended families of prodigies than should appear based on pure statistical chance. In fact, researchers have recently been able to isolate and identify a gene on chromosome 1 shared by all the prodigies and their autistic relatives that is not shared by their nonautistic family members.[23]

Where To Now?

Occasionally, when I'm feeling a little lost, I like to get a cup of tea (yes, "Tea, Earl Grey, Hot"), sit down, and try to focus on the positives. Sometimes, my positives might be as little as the fact that I got to drink my tea above a lukewarm temperature. But, usually, I'm able to uncover a few core positives in any situation, without trying to force the bits I don't know into nice, easily labeled boxes.

When trying to answer the question of whether my own children are gifted and autistic, I've found myself in the realm of statistical probabilities rather than within a neatly branded narrative. In the end, for me, the question both matters and doesn't at all. And the quest for an answer to the question "Is my gifted child autistic?" has led me in directions that have been more profound, confusing, and intriguing than I expected them to be.

In the end, the definitive answer to the question is still out there waiting to be discovered. And the journey has only just begun.

What Is a Visual-Spatial Learner?

TERESA CURRIVAN

What is the inner experience of a visual-spatial (VS) learner?

It's like a visual "knowing," where a learner (in this case, a child) is trying to find the words, math equation, musical notes, architecture modality, or any other way of putting into form what's clear in their head. Often, the vision they have in their mind's eye is clearer than they can communicate, especially to a sequential thinker who expects a child to "show their work" to be convinced that the latter knows something.

Why do VS children have a difficult time in school?

Most teaching techniques in our schools cater primarily to linear-sequential learners, whose learning typically progresses from easy to difficult material. Subjects are often taught step by step, practiced with drill and repetition, assessed under timed conditions, and then reviewed. Problem solving is taught in a systematic manner, using a series of logical steps: Memorize the math facts and then do algebra, learn to read and write and then write your own story, etc.

While these techniques work for some learners, they're counter to the VS style. More and more, I see children with varying levels of VS ability who don't yet have the sequential learning skills required early on in school. Further, VS learners tend to learn holistically. This results in their sometimes arriving at solutions without going through the usual steps. Showing their work, which is often required by teachers, may be impossible, and the child may end up not getting credit for an assignment and possibly being suspected of cheating. VS learners may succeed in solving difficult problems while finding simpler tasks a challenge, and teachers might interpret this kind of student as being obstinate or contrary.

What is the best learning environment for a VS learner?

Many parents who have highly VS children may choose to homeschool or find a school that is appropriate for VS learners. Smaller schools that are learner driven will be a better fit.

Sometimes, project-based schools work well. Ideally, students will have access to open space and nature, technology, and freedom of choice. Your child will be able to tell you if a particular learning environment works for them.

Schools that work well for VS learners will value your child's innovative ideas and support them in creating meaningful work. They will provide hands-on activities and real-world reasons to explain why anything is done, from helping to clean up and following rules to working on projects. As with all schools, make sure there is a "felt" sense that the administrators and educators involved carry out their stated values.

Whether children are schooled at home or in a brick-and-mortar school setting, these values and learning goals work for VS learners because these students are joined where they are, as opposed to being forced to reach a learning goal that may be mainstream but that doesn't necessarily suit them. At the same time, there's an expectation that they, when and if ready, will be able to adopt the more linear-sequential skills necessary to navigate the world in order to support their VS style.

The world is changing, and I believe that the VS learners among us are wired for the future. Many of them are already concerned with and ready to solve a great number of the world's problems, even those for which most of us can't imagine solutions. Meeting them where they are and helping them navigate their education while maintaining their gifts is key to helping them reach their potential, helping them grow, and helping them ultimately become contributing occupants of our planet.

Asynchronous Development Is a PITA

REBECCA FARLEY

The thing about asynchronous development is that I can't fairly write about how it looks in our house. All the stuff that would scythe right through popular one-dimensional notions of giftedness is too freaking embarrassing to my kids, and I respect them far too much to publish it.

The whole point of asynchronous development is that while some of the stuff gifted kids do makes them look absolutely amazing, quite a lot of other stuff they do—or can't do, or won't do, depending on the issue—looks pretty bloody babyish. It *is* babyish. And my kids aren't stupid; they know perfectly well they "should" have outgrown it like their age peers have, but they haven't—yet. That's not down to my coddling or their manipulation or kids these days being soft/spoiled/getting away with murder; it's just wiring.

It's integral to the full picture of what we're wrangling here, though, because the one thing we parents of gifted kids want you to know is that, honey, we ain't bragging. We cling to these words along with our gin bottles, because often the "asynchronous development" part of the gifted diagnosis is the only thing that makes our kids make *any* degree of sense.

So, instead, I'm going to share a moment from my childhood, when the asynchronicity—the all-over-the-shop development that makes gifted kids appear several ages at once—really twinkled, now that I look back through the lens of much reading.

On one hand, my parents bought me a subscription to *Reader's Digest* for my sixth birthday because I was desperate for reading material and they were desperate for me to stop asking questions—and they knew I'd love it. And, oh my god, I *did* love it. I devoured it, cover to cover, every month until we moved to Australia when I was 14 and the subscription lapsed. I can still tell you a whole stack of things I learned from *Reader's Digest*. So, on one hand, the expected precocious little smart-arse, right?

On the other hand, when my younger sisters ganged up to shame me out of thumb-sucking and sleeping with my Humpty, age 9 (first clue!), I epically

101

lost it and bashed them over the head with a broom (second clue!). This other hand—whoa. This hand was Daffy Duck, except actually dangerous. (Having been on the receiving end myself, I must say the tantrums of a three-year-old are a picnic compared to the same fury and lack of control whomping out of someone six years bigger and stronger.)

Now, I know how today's parenting forums would pile on. The "I would not stand for thats," the "completely unacceptables," the "nine years old is definitely old enough to control their tempers." It was completely unacceptable, obviously, but the point is that controlling your temper isn't about age. It's a learned skill. At nine, I had the self-control of your average three-year-old because *I had never lost my temper before.* Until that point, my parents would reasonably explain their position in any conflict and I would reasonably accept it. I'd never hit anyone; I'd never even thrown a tantrum. So, my fit that night was a double whammy: Not only had I walloped my sisters, the fact that I *could* wallop my sisters came as a giant shock to all of us. It terrified the crap out of me, and I burst into tears every bit as loud as theirs. I was *a monster*!

That's asynchronous development. That's the reason parents of gifted kids clutch their gin: At any moment, your hitherto rational, advanced, and well-adjusted child may suddenly be taken over by a foaming poltergeist of their much-younger selves—or, as in my case, a developmental stage they'd seemingly skipped altogether. (Tip: They *never* skip stages. If you think your kid has skipped a stage, by all means, read ahead and meet them wherever they are but mark the place in your book. You *will* be revisiting it, sooner or later. Sometimes much later.)

Sure, some gifted children lose their temper regularly and still take forever to learn that control. For others, it's different aspects of development that are out of whack: They can read but not write, or recite the periodic table but not toilet train, or calculate orbital trajectories in their heads but still need to co-sleep. The point is the lows that come with the highs and the vertiginous zipping between the two. One minute, your nine-year-old is waxing lyrical about David Hartman, the first blind person to graduate medical school in the United States; the next, they've lost all self-control, everyone's screaming hysterically, and you're checking the little ones for concussion.

As a parent, I have suffered this whiplash so many times it's a wonder my head is still attached. It's the thing I most wish to convey when I talk about the gifted. Sure, there's an intellectual component to the diagnosis that hogs the limelight, but as a parent, you don't really care about that. No, what keeps you awake at night is the berserker lurking behind the vocabulary, ready to leap out and wallop everyone when least expected.

That's the thing that drove me to the forums and, eventually, to my community of other, similarly traumatized parents, and it's why I'm sharing this now. If you don't get what asynchronous development is, you might not know that this is what giftedness looks like.

PART FIVE

Gifted Grows Up

Whether we gifted grown-ups arrive at our various stages of adulthood with the full knowledge of our gifted selves or show up awaiting that proverbial rude awakening, in the end, we can all rest assured that here is where we belong.

—Ann Grahl

How Will You Know a Gifted Adult When You See One?

PAULA PROBER

How do you know you're with a gifted adult?

It probably won't be obvious. And they certainly won't tell you. In fact, they may not even know themselves. They may just think they're weird. Or a little crazy. Or a lot crazy.

But there are clues.

There are certain questions that they will have trouble answering. Questions that most people think are simple. Questions like: What do you want to be when you grow up? What is your favorite book? What color do you want to paint your living room? How are you?

There are certain questions that they'll want you to ask them. Questions that most people want to avoid. Questions like: What makes life worth living? What are you reading now and how are you influenced by this particular writer? How many languages would you like to learn and why? When are you going to change career paths next and what looks good to you these days? How does the octopus express consciousness?

If you ask them if they're gifted, they'll probably say *no*. They know how much they don't know. They know people smarter than they are. They haven't invented anything *insanely great*.

They may look ungifted because they haven't become CEO of that corporation and they haven't cured cancer. They may look ungifted because they cry easily and still believe that they can change the world. They may look ungifted because they can't decide what to eat. They may look ungifted because they're easily overwhelmed by certain sounds, smells, textures, colors, chemicals, and angry humans. They may look ungifted because they dropped out of school. They may look ungifted because they forget your birthday, can't find their keys, and don't finish their 13 ongoing projects that are spread all over the house. So, it'll be hard to know if you're with a gifted adult.

But, if all else fails, look for the person with MORE.

Look for more depth, more sensitivity, more complexity. Look for more anxiety, more questioning, more researching, more existential depression, more ideas, more reading, more thinking, more compassion, more loneliness, more talking, more perfectionism, more idealism, more imagining, more laughing, more angst, more empathy, more creativity, more answers, more crying. More moreness.

And then you'll know. You're with a gifted adult. Who just might be you.

The Lonely World of the Gifted Adult—Too Smart, Too Sensitive, Too Curious

PAULA PROBER

It is part of the mythology of giftedness that supersmart people have it made. That they are successful, rich, and appreciated for their cleverness. That they don't really need much companionship because they are totally content in their labs studying fruit flies or in the library immersed in piles of books on obscure philosophical theories.

In my experience, this is not the case. These adults are often lonely. Granted, I'm a psychotherapist. Most of the gifted clients I see have lived through some sort of childhood trauma. Nevertheless, I suspect that many of the nontraumatized gifted souls among us would be telling me similar tales.

When you have a rainforest mind, it can be hard to find others who truly, deeply *get* you.[1]

Some examples:

- ✧ You are at your job, being conscientious and caring. It's important to you that your co-workers are respected and understood. You feel responsible to both the organization and the humans you supervise. Meetings are challenging. You problem solve quickly and typically end up waiting for the group to catch up. You grow tired of explaining what is obvious to you. At your evaluation, your boss tells you that co-workers say you're arrogant, condescending, and judgmental. Your boss is intimidated by you. You slow your speech and smile more. You don't share your innovative ideas or your questions. You leave homemade gluten-free cookies in the staff room. It doesn't help.

- ✧ You are in graduate school. You were so excited to join what was supposed to be a cohort of deeply intellectual lovers of research and thinkers of complex ideas. But your advisor no longer cares. They have tenure and have lost interest in academic pursuits and in you. The politics within your department is disturbing. You wonder how there can be peace on earth when your colleagues in academia can't even agree on the schedule for the next term. You feel bereft. No one shares your curiosity and your enthusiasm for Nietzsche, Virginia Woolf, quarks, Bach, the universe, and everything.

✧ You are highly intuitive. You've been an empath since you were quite young. You feel a responsibility to help others. It's hard to know if friends are attracted to you for you or if they just want you to help them heal their emphysema or contact their dead Uncle George. It's hard to have simple relationships because you can sense what others are feeling and they either put you on a pedestal or they avoid you. If you haven't been able to set healthy boundaries because you've been told that you have a gift and are responsible for sharing it, you may overwork and ignore your body's distress signals.

✧ You have a deep sense of social responsibility. It's hard not to obsess about the level of suffering that you see all around the world. Your friends and relatives tell you to lighten up and stop worrying so much. But every time an extreme weather event happens somewhere or you see a homeless person, your heart breaks.

✧ You are the parent of a gifted child. This child is bursting with energy, questions, curiosity, and emotion. You can't keep up with them and are exhausted at the end of the day. You feel a deep sense of responsibility to raise a compassionate, sensitive human. To give your child what you didn't get. Finding an appropriate school has been grueling. Other parents think it's easy to raise such a smart child. It's not.

Can you relate to any of these examples? Many of them? What can you do about the loneliness you feel? It's complicated. But, mostly, you have to know who you are. Figure out who you are. Use psychotherapy or yoga or meditation or painting or dancing or science or astrology or acupuncture or reading or hiking or music or spirituality or dark chocolate or some combination of these things. It'll require time and effort. But it'll be worth it.

Then, do activities that you love and look for the gifted folks there. Be brave and ask them for coffee/tea. They will be grateful for your courage.

The courageous rainforest-minded Charles Eisenstein has written an article that presents a fascinating perspective on living consciously in today's world. The following is a particularly uplifting and spiritually sensitive excerpt. You are not alone.

The beings we have excluded from our reality, the beings we have diminished in our perception into non-beings, they are still there waiting for us. Even with all my inherited disbelief (my inner cynic, educated in science, mathematics, and analytic philosophy, is at least as strident as yours), if I allow myself a few moments of attentive quiet, I can feel those beings gathering. Ever hopeful, they draw close to the attentiveness. Can you feel them too? Amid the doubt, maybe, and without wishful thinking, can you feel them? It is the same feeling as being in a forest and suddenly realizing as if for the first time: the forest is alive. The sun is watching me. And I am not alone.[2]

If I'm So Smart, Why Am I So Dumb?

PAULA PROBER

People may have told you that you're smart. But you may not feel smart. *Why?* Because you graduated from college with a 2.65 grade point average after changing your major five times. *Why?* Because you never finish any of the projects you start. *Why?* Because you can't decide what color to paint the bedroom and it's been three years. *Why?* Because you still daydream all the time and forget to tie your shoes. *Why?* Because you haven't won the Nobel Prize. (In fact, you haven't won anything except the spelling bee in third grade.) *Why?* Because you still cry when you gaze at the stars. *Why?* Because you know how much you don't know.

Having a rainforest mind is complicated. Let me explain.

- ✧ You have multiple interests and abilities (multipotentiality), so you may want to study many topics and not confine yourself to one field. One day you're fascinated by marine biology and the next by philosophy. How do you choose?

- ✧ Perhaps college was the first time you were challenged academically. You didn't know how to study and you couldn't stop yourself from procrastinating so your grades suffered.

- ✧ You love learning new things; but, once you learn what you need, it's time to move on. This may mean that certain projects don't look complete even though they are complete for you.

- ✧ You have high standards for your work. If you're feeling pressure to be perfect, you abandon a project because you feel paralyzed.

- ✧ You're sensitive to color so it really matters what colors you live with. Decisions, in general, are hard because you can think of way too many possibilities.

✧ Daydreaming gets a bad rap and you believed what your teachers told you about it. *Some of my best friends are daydreamers. And who has time to tie their shoes?*

✧ Winning has never been your objective.

✧ Crying is frowned upon, especially if you're a male. But you see the incredible beauty in the sky and are amazed.

People may have told you that you're smart. But you may not feel smart. That's OK. Nobody said living with a rainforest mind was going to be easy.

Beyond Achievement

ANN GRAHL

As a high school senior, they were finally nearing the place
they'd wanted to be since kindergarten—somewhere else.
Institutionalized education was never a good fit, and they
were ready to break out. But their fantasized version of
the afterlife crashed into dull reality—when their scorned
daydreaming became unappreciated vision.

They grew tired of constantly hearing how they should
be leading their life—how they weren't doing enough.
All they wanted was to live on their own terms. Pursuing
grand outcomes wasn't for them. And they'd had enough
of battling to become who everyone thought they should
be at the expense of embracing who they really were.

You see the world around you increasingly measuring giftedness in terms
of achievement or tangible output. You watch as the emphasis on
talent continues to revolve around degrees, professional status, and wealth
acquisition. And you think to yourself, those aren't my goals—that's not who
I am. Perhaps, then, I'm not really gifted; I haven't accomplished anything at
all.

But you know that isn't true. And, even if it were, you don't owe the rest of
us your brilliance or your creativity. Just as it's acceptable to aspire to greatness
and to proudly share your achievements, it's also okay to not wear your résumé
on your sleeve and to modestly walk your own chosen path or quietly enjoy a
service-centered existence.

You may have an intuition for mathematics; that doesn't mean you're
obligated to be a universally renown physicist. Or you may be a technological
whiz kid; that doesn't commit you to endless days in a computer lab. Or,
perhaps, you're a masterful writer; that doesn't dictate your future as a cutting-
edge journalist or widely published professor.

Being gifted doesn't mean that you owe a debt to the world. Possessing exceptional abilities doesn't come with a demand that you share them. Living your best life doesn't require you to follow a road paved with the skills to which you're predisposed instead of pursuing one lined with your passions.

As Ellen Fiedler notes in *Bright Minds: Uniqueness and Belonging across the Lifespan*, in a chapter discussing gifted grown-ups she calls "Invisible Ones," there are those bright adults who "quietly pursue their individual passions, even though the fruits of their labors may never be seen. This may be because they do not need external validation from others for what they do, or it may be because their creative inventions are not yet recognized by society as relevant or valuable."[3]

So, when it comes to gifted underachievement, sometimes it's not about achievement at all. Sometimes, it's about passion for passion's sake. Or about making a difference. Or about leaving an imprint that remains long after you're gone. Because, to you, these options are what represent the clearest reflections of success.

They Get It from Their Father!

ANN GRAHL

Another parent meeting, another mother declaring, "They get it from their father!"

Really? Are you sure about that?

I'm not saying that your child's father doesn't play a role in your child's giftedness. But it takes two to tango. And you, my friend, are part of the dance!

Look, I get it.

You aren't the first woman to make that proclamation. And it's not like you don't have legitimate reasons for doing so.

You don't have the creds—you were never identified, hold no higher education degrees, have no lofty career aspirations.

You were identified, excelled, achieved, and earned that PhD, but now you're "only" a mom, volunteering at your kid's school, serving on nonprofit boards, caring for an ailing parent, unable to find meaningful work that pays but honestly (and a bit embarrassingly) feeling like your life has enough meaning already.

You did lousy in school—daydreamed, checked out, prioritized romance above books. Then you moved on to college and found a way to juggle time in the library with that spent on your love life, and achieved a killer GPA in the process. But that was a fluke—anyone could have done it.

As for all those opportunities that arose as you approached graduation, they were due more to luck than to any talent you possessed. Merely the right place at the right time.

You were labeled all sorts of things—shy, sensitive, a pleaser—but never smart. And, after seeing the way smart girls were sometimes teased and made to feel unattractive, there was a part of you that was relieved. Driven by the labels bestowed, you worked diligently to mold yourself into society's notions

114

of what a girl should be. Alas, by the time adolescence hit, you were nearly a pro at hiding your braininess in an attempt to fit in.

Gifted women have their acts together. But you make a lot of mistakes, don't have any direction, can't keep a job, won't play well with others—don't, can't, won't, repeat.

Here's the thing...

Each gifted woman—just like each gifted person, or each person for that matter—is unique. And your giftedness manifests itself in its own way. Believe me, I understand the tendency to deny it or keep it hidden. But, at some point, while you're busy attributing it all to your child's father, you may be forced to concede, "They also get it from me!"

Romancing the Gift

ANN GRAHL

I sit alone, immersed in a collection of traits and characteristics—ingrained, acquired, unsuccessfully rebuffed. They represent the gifts of a lifetime that seem to have taken a lifetime to accept. Acknowledging our true selves is a journey. And, for the gifted among us, our trek may never end, as we spend countless hours exploring, cultivating, and romancing our gifts—a process especially maddening if we're late in unwrapping them.

For the "lucky" gifted folk, early identification (or any identification) was done and interventions put in place. For others, that identification never came and we found ourselves inexplicably out of step with a dance card filled with uncertainty, insecurity, and any of a hundred awkward partners that gravitated our way. We were lost souls traversing the halls of our academic and social lives. Sometimes, we drifted toward others like us—similarly confused oddballs and outcasts. Never really grasping why we were drawn to them with their quirks and unusual interests, we succumbed to their pull rather than pushing in the doors of accelerated classes and generally accepted intellectual pursuits. And there we lingered.

Until…

Higher education, a spiritual awakening, children—something eventually came into our lives and clarified our confusion. And we began to realize that the label "gifted" might actually apply to us. Not because we had achieved great things (although some of us may have) but because we came to discover that giftedness isn't merely about being brainy and wearing that brilliance on our sleeve; it's about what's underneath.

Suddenly, we were taking stock not just of who we had become but also who we once were and beginning to embrace our formerly misunderstood selves. Our enigmatic draw to others like us made greater sense—and likely continued. And the aha moments began to assemble.

Whether we gifted grown-ups arrive at our various stages of adulthood with the full knowledge of our gifted selves or show up awaiting that proverbial rude awakening, in the end, we can all rest assured that *here* is where we belong.

I've heard it said that to know one gifted person is ... well ... to know one gifted person. Perhaps that's true. But, as each additional gifted person acknowledges themself, you can glimpse others stepping into the spotlight as well, our collective dance card filling with mutual support and self-acceptance.

And it is there, together, we will shine—each of us continuing to reveal our gifts and share our unique perspective with the world.

ABOUT THE AUTHORS

Celi Trépanier, managing author for *Perspectives*, is the author of *Educating Your Gifted Child: How One Public School Teacher Embraced Homeschooling.* She writes for her own popular website, *Crushing Tall Poppies*, and serves on *The G Word* film Advisory Board. As an educator, Celi has taught in public and private schools as well as in homeschool co-ops. If you ask what her most significant accomplishment is, she may think she should say being a mom; ultimately, though, she'll proclaim it to be her role as an influential gifted advocate.

Heather Boorman, LCSW, is the founding director of Boorman Counseling in Western Wisconsin. She specializes as a trauma therapist and is an internationally recognized provider, speaker, and advocate for neurodiverse children and adults. Heather is the author of *The Gifted Kids Workbook*, writes and podcasts about raising differently wired kids at *The Fringy Bit*, and attempts to keep her sanity while parenting and homeschooling three joyfully intense gifted and 2e kids.

Stacie Brown McCullough is a writer, multipotentialite, and former secular homeschooling mom turned psychology student. She has served as GHF® periodicals board director, managing editor of *The GHF Dialogue* and *The GHF Journey*, and GHF Writing Team manager. She writes for GHF and has published multiple award-winning essays and articles appearing in college textbooks and instructor manuals by Bedford's/St. Martin's and Cengage Learning, in marketing campaigns, and in personal blogs. In addition to her writing pursuits, Stacie has founded a trio of startups, including MMc Metal Designs, LLC and a pair of gifted initiatives: The Secular Gifted Network (donated to GHF, where it was rebranded and reimagined as The GHF Forum) and SECTX Homeschool. Learn more about Stacie's pursuits at staciebrownmccullough.com.

Teresa Currivan is a licensed marriage and family therapist, parent coach, school therapist, and founder of The Right Place Learning Center. She is the author of the book *My Differently Tuned-In Child: The Right Place for Strength-Based Solutions.* She speaks about differently tuned-in children to teacher, faculty, and parent groups, and has published extensively on the topic. Teresa is recognized for developing the Currivan Protocol™ used to assess, address, cope with, and embrace symptoms and co-occurring conditions in differently wired children, such as giftedness, twice exceptionality, ADHD, dyslexia, sensory processing disorder, autism, executive functioning challenges, school refusal, defiance, depression, and anxiety. She received her MA in Counseling Psychology using Drama Therapy from the California Institute of Integral Studies in San Francisco and completed postgraduate training at The Psychotherapy Institute in Berkeley, California.

Rebecca Farley has five tertiary qualifications including a PhD in Communication. She spent nearly 20 years enrolled, working, and teaching in universities in Australia, England, and Wales, and thought that was her calling. But, after she had two children who read early, asked profound questions, and refused conventional learning, Rebecca began to research giftedness and twice exceptionality. Understanding both her kids' and her own wiring has led to a messier, more eclectic, and happier life. Rebecca lives with her husband and children, a cat, and six chickens in Queensland, Australia, and blogs about it all at *CareerusInterruptus*.

Ann Grahl is a writer, editor, consultant, and outspoken gifted advocate. Her entrepreneurial spirit and unique take on the world have led her down divergent paths. At the time of this writing, she is executive editor of GHF Press. She is also the owner of Knowledge Enrichment Enterprise, principal wordsmith at KEE Publishing, and founder of Supporting Gifted Learners. Ann finds joy in encouraging lifelong learning, amplifying unheard voices, sharing other's stories, finding common ground, and building community.

Kathleen Humble is an ADHD mum in Melbourne, Australia. She writes at *Yellow Readis* about gifted/2e homeschooling. Her book, *Gifted Myths: An Easy-to-Read Guide to the Myths, Science and History of the Gifted and Twice-Exceptional*, is available from GHF Press. She has been published in *The Victorian Writer*, *The Mighty*, and *Otherways*. Kathleen was recipient of the 2018 Writers Victoria Writeability Fellowship. In between writing and homeschooling her kids, she loves reading, sewing, and drinking big cups of tea.

Ginny Kochis is a former high school English teacher who knew everything about gifted children—until she had her own. Now an author, blogger, and gifted/2E advocate, Ginny spends most of her day keeping up with three curious, creative, intense children while equipping other moms to do the same. Ginny lives in Northern Virginia with her awesomely geeky husband and quirky kiddos. She writes from a Christian perspective on her website, *Not So Formulaic*.

Jen Merrill is a writer, musician, and gifted family advocate. The mom of two boys, she homeschooled one 2e son through high school while happily sending the other out the door every morning. Her book, *If This is a Gift, Can I Send It Back?*, struck a nerve with families; her second book on the needs of gifted parents is in progress. In addition to writing on her long-time blog, *Laughing at Chaos*, Jen has presented at SENG, NAGC, and WCGTC conferences. Jen brings both her acquired wisdom and her experience as a teacher and mentor to her work in the service of parents, guiding them into their own versions of success. Her goal is to support parents of gifted and 2e kids because they are the ones doing the heavy lifting but are too often ignored, patronized, or discredited.

Paula Prober is a psychotherapist and consultant in private practice based in Eugene, Oregon. Over the 35+ years she has worked with the gifted, Paula has been a TAG teacher and presenter at universities, webinars, podcasts, and conferences. She consults internationally with gifted adults and parents of gifted children. She has written articles on giftedness for *Psychotherapy Networker*, *Advanced Development Journal*, and the Eugene newspaper *The Register-Guard* as well as online for *Thrive Global*, *Rebelle Society*, and *Introvert Dear*. Her popular book, *Your Rainforest Mind: A Guide to the Well-Being of Gifted Adults and Youth*, was published by GHF Press. Her latest book, *Journey into Your Rainforest Mind: A Guide for Gifted Adults and Teens, Book Lovers, Overthinkers, Geeks, Sensitives, Brainiacs, Intuitives, Procrastinators, and Perfectionists*, was released in June 2019. She blogs at *Your Rainforest Mind*.

Heather Pleier is a second-generation homeschooler raising three curious, creative, outside-of-the-box kids on Long Island. They are eclectic game/interest-led/unschooly homeschoolers who dive deep into various interests and celebrate the freedom that homeschooling brings. Heather's passions include great children's literature, dark chocolate, exploration, and music. She writes at *Wonderschooling* about preserving childhood wonder and curiosity.

Gail Post, PhD, is a clinical psychologist, parenting coach, workshop leader, and writer. In clinical practice for many years, she provides psychotherapy with a focus on the needs of the intellectually and musically gifted, consultation with educators and psychotherapists, and parent coaching throughout the United States and Canada. She is the parent of two gifted young adults and served as co-chair of a gifted parents advocacy group when her children were in school. Dr. Post continues to advocate for the gifted through workshops for schools and parenting groups, written commentary, and a popular blog, *Gifted Challenges*.

Julie Schneider, MSE, MA, is a homeschooling mom, writer, community builder, advocate for neurodiversity, ally of the LGBTQ+ community, and tea-drinking yogi. She is an incessantly creative problem solver who likes to empower others. So, after listening to homeschoolers asking for a different way to investigate math, she blended her academic experience in engineering and curriculum & instruction with her life as a homeschooling parent to author *Boco Math One* and create Boco Learning.

Betsy Sproger, the owner of BJ's Homeschool, is a retired occupational therapist, veteran homeschooler, consultant, and writer. She homeschooled her 2e daughter from pre-K to college and shares their journey and favorite homeschool resources on her blog. Betsy helped her 2e daughter get into each of the colleges that she applied to and shares tips in her book *Homeschooling High School with College in Mind, 2nd edition*. Betsy also writes homeschool curriculum reviews for *The Curriculum Choice*. In addition, she offers support for special learning needs, such as ADHD and SPD, and provides a handwriting series on her blog, focusing on fun-oriented activities to build foundational skills for good handwriting. Her desire is to help parents as they homeschool their kids K–12, with a focus on homeschooling high school.

Lisa Swaboda set out at nine years old to change the world, or at least education. After 20 years of teaching and enjoying those quirky kids at school, she realized that she and her sons were quirky too. Thus, began her journey into homeschooling a gifted child and delving into what it means to be gifted for both children and adults. These days, she's still administrator of the "Gifted Adults" Facebook community she founded, where gifted adults can gather to be themselves, quirks and all. What's on the horizon? Only God knows.

NOTES

Introduction

1. Gifted Parenting Support. 2013. "The Columbus Group Conference." https:// giftedparentingsupport.blogspot.com/2013/11/the-columbus-group-conference. html.
2. Prober, Paula. 2016. *Your Rainforest Mind: A Guide to the Well-Being of Gifted Adults and Youth.* GHF Press. https://ghflearners.org/press/.

Part One: Giftedness Is

1. Worrell, Frank C., Rena F. Subotnik, Paula Olszewski-Kubilius, and Dante D. Dixson. 2018. "Gifted Students." *Annual Review of Psychology* 70, no. 1. https:// doi:10.1146/annurev-psych-010418-102846.
2. Rogers, Karen. 2017. "Worth the Effort: Finding and Supporting Twice-Exceptional Learners in School." Keynote Speech, WCGTC, Sydney.
3. Soto, Christopher J., and Joshua J. Jackson. 2013. "Five-Factor Model of Personality." In *Oxford Bibliographies in Psychology,* edited by Dana S. Dunn. Oxford: Oxford University Press. https://doi.org/10.1093/OBO/9780199828340-0120.
4. Vuyk, M. Alexandra, Thomas S. Krieshok, and Barbara A. Kerr. 2016. "Openness to Experience Rather than Overexcitabilities: Call It Like It Is." *Gifted Child Quarterly* 60, no. 3. https://doi.org/10.1177/0016986216645407.
5. Chu, Yee Han, and Bradley Meyers. 2017. "When the World Is Too Rough: Twice-Exceptional Gifted Children with Sensory Processing Disorder." Presentation, WCGTC, Sydney.
6. McBee, Matthew T., Scott J. Peters, and Erin M. Miller. 2016. "The Impact of the Nomination Stage on Gifted Program Identification: A Comprehensive Psychometric Analysis." *Gifted Child Quarterly* 60, no. 4: 258–278. https://doi. org/10.1177/0016986216656256.
7. Kula, Stacy. 2018. "Homeschooling Gifted Students: Considerations for Research and Practice." In *Curriculum Development for Gifted Education Programs,* edited by Jessica Cannaday, 151–171. Hershey: IGI Global. http://doi:10.4018/978-1-5225-3041-1.ch007.
8. Humble, Kathleen. 2017. "Alternative Education Options for Gifted and Twice Exceptional Children." Presentation, WCGTC, Sydney.

9. Guénole, Fabian, Jacqueline Louis, Christian Creveuil, Jean-Marc Baleyte, Claire Montlahuc, Pierre Fourneret, and Olivier Revol. 2013. "Behavioral Profiles of Clinically Referred Children with Intellectual Giftedness." *BioMed Research International*, July. https://www.ncbi.nlm.nih.gov/pmc/articles/PMC3722901/.

10. Gross, Miraca U. M. 2006. "Exceptionally Gifted Children: Long-Term Outcomes of Academic Acceleration and Nonacceleration." *Journal for the Education of the Gifted* 29, no. 4: 404–429. https://files.eric.ed.gov/fulltext/EJ746290.pdf.

11. Ruthsatz, Joanne, and Jourdan B. Urbach. 2012. "Child Prodigy: A Novel Cognitive Profile Places Elevated General Intelligence, Exceptional Working Memory and Attention to Detail at the Root of Prodigiousness." *Intelligence* 40, no. 5: 419–426.

12. Study of Mathematically Precocious Youth (SMPY). n.d. Vanderbilt University, Nashville. https://my.vanderbilt.edu/smpy/.

13. Schultz, Robert Arthur. 2018. "Recognizing the Outliers: Behaviors and Tendencies of the Profoundly Gifted Learner in Mixed-Ability Classrooms." *Roeper Review* 40, no. 3: 191–196. https://doi: 10.1080/02783193.2018.1469068.

14. Humble, Kathleen. 2017. "Alternative Education Options for Gifted and Twice Exceptional Children."

15. Bainbridge, Carol. 2020. "Dabrowski's Overexcitabilities in Gifted Children." Updated on June 11, 2020. https://www.verywellfamily.com/dabrowskis-overexcitabilities-in-gifted-children-1449118.

16. Perlstein, Rick. 2013. "Remembering Aaron Swartz: Each of Our Minds Contain a Universe, but How Is It That His Mind Contained Fourteen or Fifteen of Them?" *The Nation*, January 12, 2013. https://www.thenation.com/article/archive/remembering-aaron-swartz/.

Part Two: Gifted Beginnings

1. Card, David, and Laura Giuliano. 2015. "Can Universal Screening Increase the Representation of Low Income and Minority Students in Gifted Education?" Working paper 21519, National Bureau of Economic Research. https://www.nber.org/papers/w21519.

2. McBee, Matthew T., Scott J. Peters, and Erin M. Miller. 2016. "The Impact of the Nomination Stage on Gifted Program Identification: A Comprehensive Psychometric Analysis." *Gifted Child Quarterly* 60, no. 4: 258–278. https://doi.org/10.1177/0016986216656256.

3. Rimlinger, Natalie A. 2016. "Dwelling on the Right Side of the Curve: An Exploration of the Psychological Wellbeing of Parents of Gifted Children." PhD diss., The Australian National University. https://thegraysonschool.org/wp-content/uploads/n-rimlinger-abstract-dwelling-on-the-right-side-of-the-curve-1.pdf.

4. Steele-John, Jordon. 2017. "The Social Model of Disability." GreensMPs. https://jordon-steele-john.greensmps.org.au/articles/jordon-steele-john-social-model-disability.

5. Van Dam, Andrew. 2018. "It's Better To Be Born Rich than Gifted." *Washington Post*, October 9, 2018.

6. Lubinski, David, and Camilla P. Benbow. 2006. "Study of Mathematically Precocious Youth after 35 Years: Uncovering Antecedents for the Development of Math-Science Expertise." *Perspectives on Psychological Science* 1, no. 4: 316–345. https://dx.doi.org/10.1111/j.1745-6916.2006.00019.x.

7. Ford, Donna Y., Kenneth T. Dickson, Joy Lawson Davis, Michelle Trotman Scott, and Tarek C. Grantham. 2018. "A Culturally Responsive Equity-Based Bill of Rights for Gifted Students of Color." *Gifted Child Today* 41, no. 3: 125–129. https://doi.org/10.1177/1076217518769698.

8. Davis, Joy Lawson, Donna Y. Ford, James L. Moore III, and Erin Fears Floyd. 2020. "Black, Gifted, and Living in the 'Country': Searching for Equity and Excellence in Rural Gifted Education Programs." In *African American Rural Education (Advances in Race and Ethnicity in Education, Vol. 7)*, edited by C. R. Chambers and L. Crumb, pp. 39–52. Bingley, United Kingdom: Emerald Publishing Limited. https://doi.org/10.1108/S2051-231720200000007017.

9. Novak, Angela M., Katie D. Lewis, and Christine L. Weber. 2020. "Guiding Principles in Developing Equity-Driven Professional Learning for Educators of Gifted Children." *Gifted Child Today* 43, no. 3: 169–183. https://doi.org/10.1177/1076217520915743.

10. Ambrose, Don. 2020. "Interdisciplinary Exploration Clarifying Barriers Hindering Minority Achievement." *Journal of Minority Achievement, Creativity, and Leadership* 1, no. 1: 47–69.

11. Farnam Street. 2015. "Carol Dweck: A Summary of Growth and Fixed Mindsets." 2015. Blog. https://fs.blog/2015/03/carol-dweck-mindset/.

12. Myers & Briggs Foundation. 2021. https://www.myersbriggs.org/my-mbti-personality-type/mbti-basics/the-16-mbti-types.htm.

13. McIntosh, Matthew, ed. 2020. "The 'Four Temperaments' in Ancient and Medieval Medicine." *Brewminate*, October 23, 2020. https://brewminate.com/the-four-temperaments-in-ancient-and-medieval-medicine/.

14. Rivero, Lisa. 2012. "Many Ages at Once: The Science behind the Asynchronous Development of Gifted Children." *Psychology Today*. https://www.psychologytoday.com/us/blog/creative-synthesis/201201/many-ages-once.

15. Wong, Harry. 1997. *The First Days of School: How To Be an Effective Teacher*. Mountain View, CA: Harry K. Wong Publications, Inc.

16. PBS Kids. 2021. *Daniel Tiger's Neighborhood*. Fred Rogers Productions. https://pbskids.org/daniel/.

17. Bainbridge, Carol. 2020. "Dabrowski's Overexcitabilities in Gifted Children." Updated on June 11, 2020. https://www.verywellfamily.com/dabrowskis-overexcitabilities-in-gifted-children-1449118.

18. University of Cambridge. 2018. "New Brain Mapping Technique Highlights Relationship between Connectivity and IQ." https://www.sciencedaily.com/releases/2018/01/180102103313.htm.

19. National Association for Gifted Children. n.d. "Asynchronous Development." https://www.nagc.org/resources-publications/resources-parents/social-emotional-issues/asynchronous-development.

20. Bainbridge, Carol. 2020. "Dabrowski's Overexcitabilities in Gifted Children."
21. Dweck, Carol. 2014. "Developing a Growth Mindset," Stanford Alumni, YouTube. https://www.youtube.com/watch?v=hiiEcMN7vbQ.

Part Three: Gifted Gets Schooled

1. Gover, Kevin. 2016. "Choosing Our Histories." Baccalaureate address, Brown University. https://www.brown.edu/news/2016-05-28/gover.
2. Card, David, and Laura Giuliano. 2016. "Can Universal Screening Increase the Representation of Low Income and Minority Students in Gifted Education?" Working paper 21519, National Bureau of Economic Research. https://www.nber.org/papers/w21519.
3. Hardesty, Jacob, Jenna McWilliams, and Jonathan A. Plucker. 2014. "Excellence Gaps: What They Are, Why They Are Bad, and How Smart Contexts Can Address Them ... or Make Them Worse." *High Ability Studies* 25, no. 1: 71–80.
4. Post, Gail. 2017. "Gifted Underachievers Under-the-Radar." In *Gifted Underachiever*, edited by Roya Klingner, pp. 121–158. Hauppauge, NY: Nova Science Publishers.
5. Galbraith, Judy, and Jim Delisle. 2015. *When Gifted Kids Don't Have All the Answers: How to Meet Their Social and Emotional Needs.* Minneapolis: Free Spirit Publishing.
6. Cronin, Justin. 2010. *The Passage: A Novel.* New York: Ballantine Books.
7. Clynes, Tom. 2016. *The Boy Who Played with Fusion: Extreme Science, Extreme Parenting, and How to Make a Star.* New York: Houghton Mifflin Harcourt.

Part Four: 2eeek!

1. Moon, Sidney M., Sydney S. Zentall, Janice A. Grskovic, Arlene Hall, and Melissa Stormont. 2001. "Emotional and Social Characteristics of Boys with AD/HD and Giftedness: A Comparative Case Study." *Journal for the Education of the Gifted* 24, no. 3: 207–247.
2. Mullet, R., and Anne N. Rinn. 2015. "Giftedness and ADHD: Identification, Misdiagnosis, and Dual Diagnosis." *Roeper Review* 37, no. 4: 195–207.
3. Amend, Edward R., Patricia Schuler, Kathleen Beaver-Gavin, and Rebecca Beights. 2009. "A Unique Challenge: Sorting Out the Differences between Giftedness and Asperger's Disorder." *Gifted Child Today* 34, no. 4: 57–63.
4. Treffert, Darold A. 2017. "Hyperlexia: Reading Precociousness or Savant Skill?" Blog, Wisconsin Medical Society, Madison. https://www.agnesian.com/blog/hyperlexia-reading-precociousness-or-savant-skill.
5. Humble, Kathleen. 2015. "Gifted ... You Know What That Means, Right?" *Yellow Readis.* https://yellowreadis.com/2015/06/gifted-you-know-what-that-means-right.html.
6. Neihart, Maureen. 2000. "Gifted Children with Asperger's Syndrome." *Gifted Child Quarterly* 34, no. 4. https://doi.org/10.1177/001698620004400403.

7. Doobay, Alissa F., Megan Foley-Nicpon, Saba R. Ali, and Susan G. Assouline. 2014. "Cognitive, Adaptive, and Psychosocial Differences between High Ability Youth With and Without Autism Spectrum Disorder." *Journal of Autism and Developmental Disorders* 44, no. 8: 2026–2040.

8. Lord, Catherine, Michael Rutter et al. 2012. "(ADOS™-2) Autism Diagnostic Observation Schedule™," Second Edition. https://www.wpspublish.com/ados-2-autism-diagnostic-observation-schedule-second-edition.

9. AppliedBehaviorAnalysisEdu.com. n.d. https://www.appliedbehavioranalysisedu.org/how-is-ados-autism-diagnostic-observation-schedule-used-to-identify-asd/.

10. Reynolds, Cecil R., and Randy W. Kamphaus. 2015. "Behavior Assessment System for Children, Third Edition (BASC-3)." Pearson Clinical. https://www.pearsonclinical.co.uk/Psychology/ChildMentalHealth/ChildADDADHDBehaviour/basc3/behavior-assessment-system-for-children-third-edition.aspx.

11. Sparrow, Sara S., Domenic V. Cicchetti, and Celine A. Saulnier. 2016. "Vineland Adaptive Behavior Scales, Third Edition, Vineland-3." Pearson Clinical. https://www.pearsonassessments.com/store/usassessments/en/Store/Professional-Assessments/Behavior/Adaptive/Vineland-Adaptive-Behavior-Scales-%7C-Third-Edition/p/100001622.html.

12. Bright Hub Education. 2008. "What Is the Vineland Adaptive Behavior Scale?" https://www.brighthubeducation.com/special-ed-law/13506-the-vineland-adaptive-behavior-scale/.

13. Huber, D. 2007. "Clinical Presentation of Autism Spectrum Disorders in Intellectually Gifted Students." https://www.semanticscholar.org/paper/Clinical-presentation-of-autism-spectrum-disorders-Huber/ee8f30a8a33c187b88c5b5d456dad969ab5df206.

14. Neihart, Maureen. 2000. "Gifted Children with Asperger's Syndrome." *Gifted Child Quarterly* 34, no. 4. https://doi.org/10.1177/001698620004400403.

15. Neihart, Maureen. 2000. "Gifted Children with Asperger's Syndrome."

16. Burger-Veltmeijer, Agnes, and Alexander Minnaert. 2014. "Needs-Based Assessment of Students with (Suspicion of) Intellectual Giftedness and/or an Autism Spectrum Disorder: Design of an Heuristic." *Electronic Journal of Research in Educational Psychology* 12, no. 1: 211–240. https://www.researchgate.net/publication/262013191_Needs-based_assessment_of_students_with_suspicion_of_intellectual_giftedness_andor_an_Autism_Spectrum_Disorder_Design_of_an_heuristic.

17. Burger-Veltmeijer, Agnes, and Alexander Minnaert. 2014. "Needs-Based Assessment of Students."

18. Ibid.

19. Baggs, Mel. 2016. "Don't Ever Assume Autism Researchers Know What They're Doing." *Ballastexistenz Blog.* https://ballastexistenz.wordpress.com/2016/05/01/dont-ever-assume-autism-researchers-know-what-theyre-doing/.

20. Kirkovski, Melissa, Peter G. Enticott, and Paul B. Fitzgerald. 2013. "A Review of the Role of Female Gender in Autism Spectrum Disorders." *Journal of Autism and Developmental Disorders* 43, no. 11: 2584–2603.

21. Burger-Veltmeijer, Agnes, and Alexander Minnaert. 2014. "Needs-Based Assessment of Students."

22. Ruthsatz, Joanne, and Jourdan B. Urbach. 2012. "Child Prodigy: A Novel Cognitive Profile Places Elevated General Intelligence, Exceptional Working Memory and Attention to Detail at the Root of Prodigiousness." *Intelligence* 40, no. 5: 419–426.

23. Ruthsatz, Joanne, Stephen A. Petrill, Ning Li, Samuel L. Wolock, and Christopher W. Bartlett. 2015. "Molecular Genetic Evidence for Shared Etiology of Autism and Prodigy." *Human Heredity* 79, no. 2: 53–59.

Part Five: Gifted Grows Up

1. Prober, Paula. 2016. *Your Rainforest Mind: A Guide to the Well-Being of Gifted Adults and Youth.*

2. Eisenstein, Charles. 2019. "Every Act a Ceremony." https://charleseisenstein.org/essays/ceremony.

3. Fiedler, Ellen. 2015. *Bright Adults: Uniqueness and Belonging across the Lifespan,* p. 196. Tucson: Great Potential Press.

Made in United States
North Haven, CT
29 December 2021

13756976R00075